A Language of Contemporary Architecture

As a way to understand the contemporary project in architecture, this book provides an index of ideas, theories, projects, and definitions that string into a methodology for evaluating the contemporary language of architecture described as "contemporism" through a review of topology (form) and typology (system and elements).

The contemporary project has been trying to answer the post-modern question of how to move beyond modernism through a thread of architectural styles that tried to respond to deficiencies from the modern promise and contextual changes. Yet, the question remains, should this ongoing struggle to move beyond modernism be a stylistic battle? Has the present architectural practice ever left the modernist tendencies, and is there a structure for a contemporary language in architecture? This book presents a collection of highly illustrated projects that have worked under these parameters to break away from modernism in order to present a holistic integration of topology and typology as a language for "contemporism." The index is illustrated with individual spreads, which can be read sequentially or independently, and encourages the reader to make their own connections. It also includes interviews and contributions from Toyo Ito, Anthony Vidler, Ben van Berkel, Christian Kerez, and Greg Lynn.

This book is essential reading for undergraduate and graduate students in architecture.

PRAUD was founded by Dongwoo Yim and Rafael Luna in 2010, with offices in Boston and Seoul. Their theoretical investigations and criticism of the contemporary language in architecture spans over a decade of academic appointments, completed international projects, awarded competitions, and multiple publications and exhibition roles. This led them to win awards such as the Architectural League Prize in 2013, the DAM book award, and exhibited internationally at MoMA, Venice Biennale, and Seoul

Biennale on several occasions. They curated the "Cities Exhibition" at the 2019 Seoul Biennale, co-directed the Future School Summer School program for the 2020 Venice Biennale Korean Pavilion, and served as guest editors for the October 2021 issue of AD magazine entitled "Production Urbanism: the Meta-Industrial City."

Dongwoo Yim is the co-founder of PRAUD and an assistant professor at Hongik University Graduate School of Architecture and Urban Design. He received his master's degree at Harvard University and a bachelor's degree at Seoul National University and is currently a Ph.D. candidate from Università della Svizzera Italiana. He is the winner of the Architectural League Prize 2013. He is the author of "Pyongyang, and Pyongyang After," and "(Un) Precedented Pyongyang," and co-author of the "North Korean Atlas" and "I Want to be METROPOLITAN." His works have been exhibited worldwide including the Golden Lion-winning Korean Pavilion in Venice Biennale 2014, the Museum of Modern Art in New York, and DNA Galerie in Berlin. Dongwoo has also held academic positions at the Rhode Island School of Design from 2011 through 2017, and visiting assistant professor at Washington University in St. Louis in 2016. He was the curator of Pyongyang Sallim and Letters to the Mayor: Seoul + Pyongyang in the 2017 Seoul Biennale of Architecture and Urbanism and the co-curator of the Cities Exhibition in the 2019 SBAU.

Rafael Luna is the co-founder of the architecture firm PRAUD and Senior Lecturer at the University of Technology Sydney. He received a Master of Architecture from the Massachusetts Institute of Technology (2010), and his Ph.D. in Architecture from L'Accademia di architettura dell'Università della Svizzera italiana (2022). Luna is the award winner of the Architectural League Prize 2013, and his work has been exhibited at the MoMA, Venice Biennale, and Seoul Biennale. Luna was a co-curator of the Cities Exhibition for the 2019 Seoul Biennale. He has professional experience from the offices of Toyo Ito and Associates, KPF, Ateliers Jean Nouvel, Martha Schwartz Partners, dECOI, Sasaki Associates, and Machado and Silvetti. He served as an assistant professor at Hanyang University from 2018 to 2022, previously teaching at the Rhode Island School of Design. His writings have been published in journals such as G+L, Topos, MONU, SPACE, IntAR Journal, and he was a guest co-editor for AD magazine's September 2021 issue "Production Urbanism: The Meta-Industrial City." He is the co-author of "I Want to Be Metropolitan" and the "North Korean Atlas."

A Language of Contemporary Architecture
An Index of Topology and Typology

By PRAUD
Rafael Luna and
Dongwoo Yim

Designed cover image: © HongKim

First published 2023
by Routledge
4 Park Square, Milton Park, Abingdon, Oxon OX14 4RN

and by Routledge
605 Third Avenue, New York, NY 10158

Routledge is an imprint of the Taylor & Francis Group, an informa business

© 2023 Rafael Luna and Dongwoo Yim

The right of Rafael Luna and Dongwoo Yim to be identified as authors of this work has been asserted in accordance with sections 77 and 78 of the Copyright, Designs and Patents Act 1988.

All rights reserved. No part of this book may be reprinted or reproduced or utilised in any form or by any electronic, mechanical, or other means, now known or hereafter invented, including photocopying and recording, or in any information storage or retrieval system, without permission in writing from the publishers.

Trademark notice: Product or corporate names may be trademarks or registered trademarks, and are used only for identification and explanation without intent to infringe.

British Library Cataloguing-in-Publication Data
A catalogue record for this book is available from the British Library

Library of Congress Cataloging-in-Publication Data
Names: Luna, Rafael, 1984– author. | Yim, Dongwoo, author.
Title: A language of contemporary architecture: an index of topology and typology / by PRAUD, Rafael Luna and Dongwoo Yim.
Description: Abingdon, Oxon: Routledge, 2023. | Includes index. |
Identifiers: LCCN 2022046650 | ISBN 9781032245409 (hardback) | ISBN 9781032245386 (paperback) | ISBN 9781003279198 (ebook)
Subjects: LCSH: Architecture, Modern–20th century–Themes, motives. | Architecture, Modern–21st century–Themes, motives. | Architecture, Modern–20th century–Philosophy. | Architecture, Modern–21st century–Philosophy.
Classification: LCC NA680 .L84 2023 |
DDC 724/.6–dc23/eng/20221109
LC record available at https://lccn.loc.gov/2022046650

ISBN: 978-1-032-24540-9 (hbk)
ISBN: 978-1-032-24538-6 (pbk)
ISBN: 978-1-003-27919-8 (ebk)

DOI: 10.4324/9781003279198

Typeset in Panama
by codeMantra

Contents

9	**PROLOGUE**
10	*The New "Real": Toward Reclaiming Materiality in Contemporary Architecture* by Toyo Ito
19	**INTRODUCTION**
20	*Introduction by PRAUD*
28	Modern or Contemporary
30	Facadism
32	The Third Typology
34	First Typology: Primitive Hut
36	Taxonomy of Elements
38	Second Typology: System
40	Third Typology: Form
42	*The Third Typology Reconsidered.* by Anthony Vidler
64	**Index Part 1 TOPOLOGY**
66	*Did Technology Kill the Box?* Interview with Ben van Berkel
70	*On Topology* Interview with Greg Lynn
76	**Mug = Donut**
78	**Animate Form**
80	**De-form**
82	**Soft Topologies**
84	**Dis-orientation**
86	**Topology and Intent**
88	**Formalism**
90	**Pure Form**
92	**Contextualization**
94	**Legal Contextualization**
96	**Urban Contextualization**
98	**Contextual Transformation**
100	**Open Context**
102	**Closed Context**

104	Connotation / Denotation
106	Sign Language
108	Semiotics
110	Signified and Signifier
112	Adopted Form
114	Courtyards
116	Absolute Form
118	Collective Form: (Compositional Form)
120	Collective Form: (Megaform)
122	Collective Form: (Group Form)
124	City as Topologies
126	Hybrid Form
128	Found Form
130	Form over Function
132	"We'll Have One of Each"
134	Programmatic Element
136	Form as System
138	Parts to Whole
140	Figure-Ground
142	Groundfigure
144	Unanchored
146	Ground
148	Groundscape
150	The Oblique
152	Figure-Sky
154	Urban Frame
156	Figure No Ground
158	Topologies of Containment
160	Tunnel Third Space
162	Lawn Third Space

164	**Index Part 2**	**TYPOLOGY**
166	*Rule of Engagement* Interview with Christian Kerez	
176	Façade Design – Five Points of Architecture	
178	Interchangeable Façades	
180	Decon-textual	
182	Separation of Roles by Elements	
184	Beyond Modernism	
186	In-tension	

188	Façade Roles
190	Tube Frame
192	Structural Effect
194	Material Logic
196	Structural Ornament
198	Holistic Ornament
200	Hyperbolic Paraboloids
202	Lofting
204	Wall Spacing
206	Four Walls
208	One Wall
210	Fluid Surface
212	Fluid Walls
214	Dom-ino Slab
216	Continuous Slab
218	Single Surface
220	Ribbon
222	Column Expression
224	Column Frame
226	Strapping Column
228	Table Column
230	Tables
232	Spatial Column
234	Programmable Column
236	Room Column
238	Flat Column
240	Modular Column
242	Object Column
244	Skewer Core
246	Stretching Core
248	Siamese Core
250	Structuralist Core
252	Metabolic Core
254	Infrastructural Core
256	Tentacle Core
258	Façade Core
260	Obese Core
262	Modular Stacking
264	Modular System
266	Prefab Stacking

268	I-Beam Stacking
270	Preform Stacking
272	Interlocking
274	Ground Stacking
276	Coursing
278	Found System

280	**TO/TY as Methodology**
282	*Concluding Analysis and Speculations*
288	Six Experiments
292	Three-dimensional Structural Pattern – Dubai Pavilion
294	Topology
296	Structural Ground – Gwangju Library
298	Topology
300	Figure over Ground
304	French Fries Sandwich
308	Horizontal Third Space
312	Vertical Third Space
314	Topology
316	Four Houses
320	Massing - Intent
322	Massing - Strategy
324	System
326	Production Of Third Space
328	*Beyond Modernism*
	In conversation with Toyo Ito
334	*References Per Spread*
339	*Index*

Pro-logue

The New "Real"
Toward Reclaiming Materiality in Contemporary Architecture

By Toyo Ito

June 2006 found me on the ground floor of the Neue Nationalgalerie in Berlin, standing atop a white mound some 1,000 m² in size whose undulating surface was crowded with a sea of people. More than a dozen artists had displayed artworks they created in response to this mound. Some had taken it as their unframed "canvas" and spray-painted bright colors directly on the white ground; others bored holes in it, crawled up inside and proceeded to paint murals that recalled primitive man drawing cave paintings; still others excavated hollows (something like capsule hotel rooms or impromptu shelters devised by homeless persons) in which to install their work, demanding that visitors sit or lie down in order to appreciate the below.

Naturally, not all artists elected to work in response to the mound. There were those who wholly ignored it or simply hung their work on walls the same as ever. Nonetheless, the undulating floor surely did elicit different responses from artists than the typical "white cube" interior.

Why, then, did I design such a mound? Because I wanted to transform Mies' flat floor and soften the rigid near-perfection of his grid system.

Mies van der Rohe is considered the creator of the uniform grid that dominated twentieth-century architecture. The Neue Nationalgalerie completed in 1968 is a work from the very last years of a life spent entirely in pursuit of grids, and indeed may be said to be the summation of his grid thinking. With its large flat roof floated upon a raised base, its square plan encased in glass on all four sides, its symmetry of cruciform columns with its core element placed exactly in the center – this is a temple, a paean to twentieth-century Euclidean geometry.

Yet the more total the grid system, the more perfectly pure the geometric space, the less I felt like putting up partition walls in keeping with that geometry. No, I wanted to dissolve its modular regularity, to transform its floor into rolling hills. Not

DOI: 10.4324/9781003279198-1

to destroy Mies' space or oppose it, but simply to try to shift it into a different orientation – a nudge toward what I now call the "emerging grid." The architecture I now seek pushes Euclidean geometry in the direction of nonlinear geometries based on nature, because I feel that people are losing their sensitivity and vitality within such pervasive grid-form urban environments and architectural spaces.

Uniform grid space characterizes most cities today – New York, Chicago, Los Angeles, Toronto, Beijing, Shanghai, Paris, Singapore, Tokyo – all virtually indistinguishable inorganic continuums of glass and steel, utterly artificial environments bearing no relation to nature. There work countless people, driven by the dictates of economics and information, their lives spent looking away from real material things as they fret and fritter their days in abstract boxes possessed by the abstract machinations of money.

Was the final aim of Mies' famous aphorism "Less is more" to have people live in a Cartesian vacuum? The vision of unemotional, never-sweating professionals gazing silently at computer monitors in spaces impossibly divorced from nature may well be the ultimate, most beautifully abstract goal of the twentieth century, yet beyond that what is there to see but the ruins of Modernism devoid of even those cool-and-dry workaholics?

I began to want to show the material strength in such abstract, inorganic spaces only after groundbreaking at the Sendai Mediatheque. The building is simple in composition: 13 randomly placed "tubes" made of steel pipes support 7 layered square "plates," creating an empty interior penetrated by large trunk-like columns and encircled by glass; each "honeycomb panel" floor comprises dual 50-m^2 steel sheets that sandwich polygonal ribbing, effectively eliminating the need for beams. The strong contrast between organic-shaped "tubes" and thin, highly abstract "plates" almost seems to plant a grove of trees across an otherwise manmade expanse. Or rather, it suddenly brings pure geometries into nature and sets them up in striking counterpoint. Like a cube cut out of a forest-like continuum to the actual site and programmatic conditions, hence all façades are simply lopped off cross-sections.

Humans who once lived in the caves and forests of the natural world used to cut down trees to build shelters for themselves. Such shelters became "architecture" only after giving them independent form and geometric order. When Marc-Antoine Laugier describes the primitive country hut as "le modèle sur lequel on a imaginé toutes les magnificences de l'Architecture" (Essai sur l'architecture: nouvelle édition, 1755, p.9) I read this to mean that the essence of architecture since ancient times has been "an independent formal order that stemmed from the natural world." Twentieth-century Modernism replaced the order of round columns and pediments to establish an order of simple, abstract perpendicular lines. Yet even in Mies' Neue Nationalgalerie we have already seen how this order derived from a uniform grid totally independent from nature.

However, we might just as easily say that the "tubes" introduce a different geometry into an otherwise pure Cartesian coordinate grid, and using gigantic steel members no less. Thus, both in Berlin and in Sendai, contrary to the historical order of architecture taking shape in nature, I attempted the reverse process: to induce nature out of built forms, as well as to inject materiality into "Less is more" space, precisely in order to return some living reality to the void of economics and data. What we might call a "new real" in materiality beyond Modernism. No mere nostalgic or superficial touches, my challenge was to envision a whole new way of architecture.

In attempting to regain material power in architecture, structure offers important clues. Like the skeletal and muscular systems of the human body, structural members physically support buildings by directly transmitting stresses. In past architecture, however, these essentially dynamic flows were sealed within the static geometries of formal architectural orders, as when Vitruvius likened balance in symmetrical stasis to the body circumscribed within circles and squares despite the instable balancing of the body in motion. Likewise, twentieth-century uniform grid architecture concertedly forced stresses to flow uniformly along perpendicular lines. Yet in either age, the dynamism of stress flows remained concealed within classic geometrical orders.

Whereas computer technologies are now liberating architecture from Euclidean geometries, they are enabling the realization of the unstable fluidity of the moving body and the complex balance of growing plant life in architectural space.

The structural engineers I have collaborated with since Sendai – Mutsuro Sasaki, Cecil Balmond, Masato Araya, Masahiro Ikeda – all possess a gift for structural analyses based in nonlinear mathematics. These men are creating structures out of the complex, dynamic interplay of forces – "fluid body

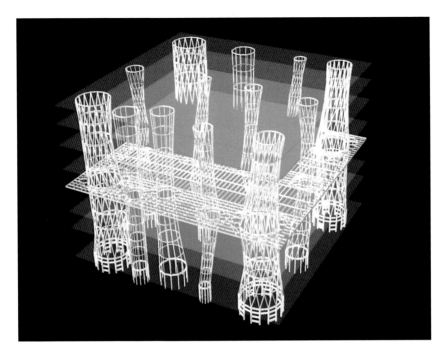

SENDAI MEDIATHEQUE, Toyo Ito, Sendai, Japan. 2001
The structural engineers I have collaborated with since
Sendai – Mutsuro Sasaki, Cecil Balmond,

architectures" – that would have been inconceivable, let alone attainable last century. In Sasaki's designs for the Building for Island City Central Park "GRIN" or the Crematorium in Kakamigahara, for instance, he realized continuous spaces within three-dimensionally curved "free-form shells." Common to both these projects was how readily he was able to analyze structures directly from the shape of virtually any curved surfaces we could imagine. Of course, he would first rely on his own structural expert's intuition to tell him which shapes looked potentially viable, then coax and correct the forms in the proper direction. Yet even so, his approach is nothing like heretofore prevailing methods; up until now, before entering into simulations, the structural engineer would first establish conventional structural schema, analyses being possible only within those formats. In other words, no matter how freely the architect might imagine his forms, he would first have to somehow fit them into the engineer's pre-determined frameworks. With Sasaki's new methods, however, the available frameworks have so

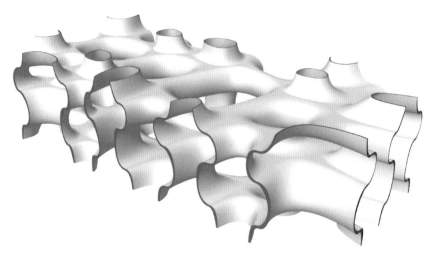

National Taichung Theater, Toyo Ito, Taichung, Taiwan. 2016
As Sasaki explains

greatly expanded that the architect has all the freedom he could possibly want.
　　As Sasaki explains,
　　　　However, taking the design as the given conditions, with the aim of obtaining it as the resulting structure, would be an original structural design procedure for creating a structure that conforms to the desired design while following mechanical principles. A process of directly finding the optimum structural type and shape that satisfies the design parameters of the desired space is called design analysis, or shape analysis. Utilizing structural mechanics as an integrated design method, this process is completely opposite to the sequential approach of conventional structural analysis, and is therefore a kind of reverse analysis."
　　　　(Flux Structure: TOTO Shuppan, 2005, pp. 49-51)
The continuous shell in Island City is a good example of this reverse analysis. Here three shells with open centers alternate in a convex-concave sequence describing something like a spiral, a major departure from the conventional "shell" typology. Study for his three-part shell began with rendering a visible model, which was then measured in order to digitize data and ultimately produce

a structural simulation. As a result, we can experience a very dynamic topological space.

Araya's structural analysis for the TOD'S Omotesando Building followed a similar process. The image of overlapping tree silhouettes was first put forth from my side, as the architect, whereupon he proceeded to see how the stresses would flow in such a complex network of crisscrossed branches. All the branching shapes were immediately digitized to create a simulation, which was then repeatedly amended and adjusted toward an equilibrium within the chosen parameters; each partial change in the shape of a single branch would affect the equilibrium of all the other branches – hence the permeations were potentially limitless.

Araya's efforts at analyzing complex stress flows would have been next to impossible a decade ago. Computer technology has revolutionized our ability to dissect structural forms – columns, beams, braces, walls.

The treeform structural members in TOD'S are symbolic in the sense that each tree yields its own equilibrium yet never repeats, a rich variation of forms that reflects the biodiversity of the natural world.

Cecil Balmond, the structural engineer who collaborated on the Serpentine Gallery Pavilion 2002 in London's Kensington Gardens, is even more of a philosopher than he is a technical whiz. Indeed, he calls himself a "natural philosopher". He takes great interest in the autonomic shaping of the natural world, how its component molecules behave and bring together various structures.

His conceptual approach to drawing a rectangle, for instance, does not seek a constant form, but rather "the energy of one line in relation to the energy of the other line" which he pursues as "a ratio or frozen time constricting movements in space" ("Cecil Balmond Meets Toyo Ito," a+u issue 404, May 2004, p.46) Thus, to him, geometry always consists in the tracks of moving points: the application of certain parameters to the endless multiplicity of countless streaming points and the line traces they leave, rules governing directions and intersections that inform his concept of architectural structure. What up to now have been pure shapes – circles, squares, and cubes – he totally reconceived as select frozen moments in the on-going motions of points.

The surface of the Serpentine Pavilion, seemingly a random network of tangled lines, formed a structure of flat steel bars according to Balmond's precise algorithms that inset squares in rotating concentric succession, this dynamic twist transforming the pure geometric shape into a spiraling environment.

"As the lines race over the plane shooting down the sides at angles only to kick back through the base and rise up the other side, the surface becomes a mesh of circuits, going nowhere and yet at the same time moving towards everywhere. Normal extension ceases; we are in a time capsule. We occupy space that undermines the idea of limit, denying skin to volume" (Cecil Balmond quoted in "Serpentine Gallery Pavilion 2002: Toyo Ito with Arup," telescoweb. com).

For a fact, the experience of being inside the Pavilion with no visible columns and beams or windows and doors, none of the usual hierarchy of architectural forms, is that of space itself – an ever-fluctuating, self-recursive abstract space whose interior and exterior are contiguous, not at all organic yet filled with a curious vitality.

Two yet-uncompleted projects, the Project for Forum for Music, Dance and Visual Culture Centre in Ghent and Project for Taichung Metropolitan Opera House, utilize similar structural systems to create maze-like continuums of three-dimensionally curved spaces, all very complex in appearance yet based on clear and simple principles. Two parallel horizontal planes divided into uniform grids, each with alternating circles circumscribed in checkerboard fashion, are positioned so that the circles above and below are one square out of congruity with each other; these circles are then interconnected as if via resilient membranes, the three-dimensionally curved surfaces of the "membranes" dividing the floor plan into distinct spaces. By further stacking this system in a vertical direction, the articulated spaces respectively form continuous vertical and horizontal "tubes." If the grid and circles are kept uniform in size, then all tubular spaces would also be equal, but varying the size and shifting their centers yields a complex array of irregular spaces.

We have dubbed this the "emerging grid": a system by which a uniform grid is manipulated to yield a continuum with a three-dimensionally curved shell; a method for transforming simple regular spaces into complex spaces rich in variation, hard inorganic space into supple organic space.

During the Ghent competition, we experimented with numerous trial-and-error variations using this process, arriving at the requisite 1800-seat concert hall, dance/orchestra rehearsal studios and rooms for workshops. But instead of a conventional auditorium, we proposed that the hall be an extension of exterior urban space, so that the light-hearted ease of outdoor concerts carries over into the interior. Or to put it another way, we attempted to convolutedly "network" the street into the building, with spaces therein that could be used for music and dance performances. It was the "emerging grid" system that allowed us to realize a volumetrically interconnected image of the street capable of fulfilling all the preconditions.

The tubes that run vertically in Sendai span the entire Ghent project horizontally and vertically. The space is continuous throughout; though, as in Sendai, the tubes are cut off to conform to the site, exposing cross-sections to the perimeter as curved waveforms – as if in analogy to the organ passages that run through the human body. Are the intestines and esophagus internal or external organs? One might ask the same thing about the "sound tubes" in Ghent. It is amazing to see how submitting a uniform grid to a series of algorithms can deliver such organic spatial qualities.

Likewise in Taichung, albeit carried further than in Ghent, the three theater spaces required for opera and drama seemed to demand self-contained conventional spaces, yet by utilizing the "emerging grid" we were able to create spaces closer to caverns than tubes – and infused with energy.

In any case, surface network structural systems as in TOD'S or the Serpentine Pavilion now applied to three-dimensional surfaces in Island City or Kakamigahara as total spatial network systems.

Most of the projects we have done since Sendai have been very likely unrepeatable "handmade" efforts that involved reinforcing struts molded to complex three-dimensionally curved surfaces, steel ribs and plates requiring enormous numbers of precision welds, pieces of glass cut to different irregular shapes that then had to be individually fitted into concrete frames – all incredibly demanding operations. The sheer amount of energy and exactitude invested in realizing these "problematic" buildings is testament to our aims to find a "new real" material power in architecture.

The various specific projects we have looked at thus far all exemplify a common thesis that can be summed up as follows:

1. Liberate architecture from staid prevailing forms via dynamic stress flows.
2. Transform Modernist "less-is-more" minimal spaces into primal "real places" in tune with nature.

Contemporary architecture – and especially Japanese contemporary architecture – is almost entirely concerned with Modernist sophistication. Minimal and stoic, many are the buildings that showcase a pure geometric beauty, but do they really invigorate people? As all too often art history shows, in some ways, nothing spoils creative impulses as much as sophistication.

In today's world, where buildings have been reduced to mere "consumables" in the scheme of economics and information media, what we seek in architecture are spaces that are truly alive, that actually engage us physically. Or as I would sum up in two dictums: "Fluid spaces where we can feel the dynamic stress flows" and "Nature-conscious spaces with primitive qualities akin to tree houses and caves." Not that I advocate a return to the past, I'm staking the latest technologies on the "new real" dream beyond Modernism.

(translated by Alfred Birnbaum)

Intro-
duction

Introduction by PRAUD

The contemporary project has been trying to answer the post-modern question on how to move beyond modernism. This preoccupation does not come from an egocentric notion of novelty, but it rises from an understanding of a contextual change and an architectural response that can address such technical, economic, and social change. Modernism itself comes as a diagrammatic response to a contextual change during the first half of the twentieth century. Fascinated by the Fordist approach to mass production, Le Corbusier presented the diagram for the domino system, which became the essential diagram for the reconstruction of war-torn countries across Europe, and an initial globalized standard for urban development. The system has been so efficient and widely accepted that no significant diagrams have challenged it sufficiently even though we have seen significant changes in construction methods, material technology, visualization technology, climate change, unstable political and socio-economical scenes where the modernist system no longer applies. The contemporary response to the post-Fordist era or fourth industrial revolution that we are in has generated projects that tackle new spatial configurations through the use of new construction systems as seen by Toyo Ito or Kengo Kuma, new programmatic environments of provocation by OMA, new fluidity in space by UN Studio or Zaha Hadid Architects, new use of materials that generate new phenomena and effects like Herzog and de Meuron or Peter Zumthor, and new urban massings that challenge the public realm by MVRDV just to mention a few.

The Problem with Styles

Historically, the critical move from modernism led to a successive thread of architectural styles that tried to respond to deficiencies from the modern promise. Each new style represented a new canon that strove to move away from the previous projects as the new interpretation of contemporary practice. Postmodernism, for example,

20   DOI: 10.4324/9781003279198-2

tried to revive agendas of symbolism in the architectural language which architects like Michael Graves or Ricardo Bofill fulfilled in their seminal projects. Kenneth Frampton responded to the postmodern attitude in his essay "Towards a Critical Regionalism: Six Points for an Architecture of Resistance" by addressing the need to reevaluate the global trends as respondents to the local culture and parameters. Out of modernism, brutalism also emerged as a tectonic response for new systems of construction and expression. Modernist city planning was also criticized by structuralism and the metabolist, who devised projects that embed an element of time and growth, a more organic aggregation to the city rather than the sterile response from Congrès International d'Architecture Moderne(CIAM) planning. High-tech architects appeared as late modernists, expressing new materials and construction methods as the expression of the building in order to provide a free interior flexible space rather than the modernist "free plan."

This battle of styles is an ongoing challenge to define the contemporary project while providing an all-encompassing language that disseminates into all design environments and scales, just as modernism did. For example, Parametricism produces a design strategy seen in the works of Zaha Hadid Architects ranging from furniture to architecture to urban design through a computational logic of form-making. Yet, the question remains, should this ongoing struggle to move beyond modernism be a stylistic battle? Has the present architectural practice ever left the modernist tendencies, and how can we define Contemporary Architecture through a non-stylistic approach? Is there a structure for a contemporary language in architecture? Just as Modernism can be dissected through its elements and systems, should there be a comparative approach for understanding Contemporarism? How can a critical reading of Contemporary Architecture occur when much of this distinction is lost in the contemporary practice and more significantly in the architectural education, due to the misconstrued allure of new fabrication technologies, or parallel agendas such as social equity, that mislead the denotation of "good" in architecture as a socio-technical achievement or innovation, while the inherent architectural system remains that of modernism? All these questions make this an imminent discussion for answering: does Contemporary Architecture exist not as a temporal trait but as an architectural method?

The Quandary of Contemporary

In the hypothetical of the Cathedral of Santa Maria del Fiore and Villa Savoye being built now, would both projects be considered Contemporary Architecture? If contemporary is to be understood as a condition of time, then yes, they would both be considered Contemporary Architecture in a temporal sense. Yet, even if these two buildings were built at the same time, it is evident that they do not follow the same logic of assemblage, as they are bound to different stylistic parameters. Style has a temporal value that reflects the socio-technical conditions of a period, and, therefore, following a style classifies a piece of architecture under set rules, regardless of the time when it is built. For example, even though Gothic architecture had its prime between the twelfth and sixteenth centuries in Europe, the Washington National Cathedral in Washington DC built in the twentieth century can still be read as Gothic architecture. Built outside of its stylistic context, style only has a symbolic meaning, since the reproduction of style with new means of construction can only reflect an ornamental expression. If style has such intrinsic properties of time, then Contemporary Architecture cannot be purely assessed by **when** it was built, but rather **how** it was built.

Typology beyond Style

"In the postmodern period, theorists reconsidered the notion of type as the essence of architecture, seen in some cases as comparable to linguistic deep structure."[1]

Without getting into the semiotics of architecture as a language, there is a grammatical composition to architecture, an inherent structure for how to construct an environment and space. This is not stylistic but typological. Typology in itself has an extended lineage of study as a way of understanding the root of architecture by the likes of Alan Colquhoun, Giulio Carlo Argan, Rafael Moneo, Anthony Vidler, among others. There is a distinction to be made within this lineage that arises from the word "type." Type is theorized in the eighteenth century by Antoine-Chrysostome Quatremère de Quincy in his *Dictionnaire historique d'architecture*.[2]

---

1   Nesbitt, Kate. *Theorizing a New Agenda for Architecture: An Anthology of Architectural Theory 1965-1995*. Princeton Architectural Press, Princeton, NJ, 2008, p. 240.

2   Quincy Quatremère de. *Dictionnaire Historique D'architecture*. Librairie D'Adrien Le Clere, Paris, France, 1832.

Topologies,
PRAUD, 2016

Topology blocks,
PRAUD, 2016

Quatremère de Quincy would begin to explain its etymology from a Greek origin, τύπος, used to describe the mold for producing a sculpture or work of art. He theorized that type represented more the rule rather than the image to be copied. "Les mot type présente moins l'image d'une chose à copier ou à imiter complètement, que l'idée d' un élément qui doit lui-même servir de règle au modèle."[3] This interpretation was promoted by Giulio Carlo Argan in his essay "On the Typology of Architecture,"[4] and by Rafael Moneo in "On Typology."[5] Both essays (Argan's and Moneo's) would present the case for Typology as a conceptual irreducible inherent structure. A variation of this concept lies in Alan Colquhoun's explanation of the designer's intuition to produce "type-solutions" when lacking in critical scientific methods for solving complex problems.[6] The design method relies on the paradoxical confrontation between biotechnical determinism and free expression (intuition). In the design process, it is inconceivable to be able to supply all the parameters for a problem, and Typology fills in that gap. Typology, in this case, is intuitive and analogous to the inherent structure.

Elements, System, and Form

It is important to note that both Typology as "designer's intuition" and Typology as "inherent structure" separate themselves from Typology as function, which was ruled out by Rossi.[7] Yet one possible variation for the definition of Typology that offers such clarity comes from the re-interpretation of Anthony Vidler's "The Third Typology."[8] Vidler classifies the existence of a first Typology based on elements of architecture (Laugier's Primitive Hut), a second Typology deriving from the systems of fabrication (Le Corbusier's Maison Domino), and the third Typology as an emergent relationship between city

---

3   Quincy Quatremère de. *Dictionnaire Historique D'architecture*. Librairie D'Adrien Le Clere, 1832, p. 629.

4   Argan, Giulio Carlo. "On The Typology of Architecture." *Theorizing a New Agenda for Architecture: An Anthology of Architectural Theory, 1965–1995*, edited by Kate Nesbitt, Princeton Architectural Press, New York, NY, 1996, pp. 242–246.

5   Moneo, Rafael. "On Typology." *A Journal for Ideas and Criticism in Architecture*, vol. 18, 1978, pp. 23–45.

6   Colquhoun, Alan. "Typology and Design Method." *Theorizing a New Agenda for Architecture: An Anthology of Architectural Theory 1965–1995*, edited by Kate Nesbitt, Princeton Architectural Press, New York, NY, 1996, pp. 250–257.

7   Rossi, Aldo. *The Architecture of the City*. MIT Press, 2007.

8   Vidler, Anthony. "The Third Typology." *Theorizing a New Agenda for Architecture: An Anthology of Architectural Theory 1965–1995*, edited by Kate Nesbitt, Princeton Architectural Press, New York, NY, 1996, pp. 260–263.

and form (Aldo Rossi and Leon Krier). While these three typologies are defined separately, when combined they offer the possibility of architectural production deprived of style. While form is understood as a separate Typology, its role is to contextualize architecture to a site through its deformations, creating spatial relationships between the city and architecture, and within itself through its massing composition. Due to a new mathematical understanding of our world as topological, this third Typology could be renamed as topology, while elements and systems can remain as Typology. The method of composing a topology and then assessing what elements and systems relate best to the topology is a potential method for Contemporary Architecture, beyond a modern framework, beyond style.

How to Use This Book

This book is meant to illustrate references of precedent projects for understanding a topological/ typological approach to Contemporary Architecture. Rather than a textbook in the traditional sense, this book organizes the narrative of Topology and Typology through sections rather than chapters. Toyo Ito describes a new conception of the grid as a divergence from modernism. A proposal for a topological/ typological method to Contemporary Architecture is introduced through illustrations that explain the references described in "The Third Typology." Anthony Vidler offers a review of "The Third Typology" as a way to begin the book with a theoretical background. A **Topology** section introduces issues of form in architecture, which are discussed through interviews with Greg Lynn and Ben van Berkel. A **Typology** section diagrams projects that have deviated from the modernist agenda by inflicting modern elements, or proposing new systems. Sou Fujimoto and Christian Kerez provide their perspective on the matter. A **Methodology** section explains the integration between Topology and Typology as a holistic method for Contemporary Architecture.

Each section is illustrated with spreads, which can be read sequentially or independently. The reader is encouraged to form their own associations through the connection of spreads within each section.

Spreads

Each spread is composed of curated examples that aim at explaining a concept within each section of the book. The introductory section exhibits key projects for understanding each of the Typology definitions that have been interpreted from Vidler's "The Third Typology," as this is the premise for proposing a contemporary method for architecture. The section on Topology has been curated with projects that describe different roles for FORM in architecture, such as contextualization, the third space, issues of form versus function, form as a system, form and the city, form and ground. The spreads on the Typology section present projects that have attempted to break modernism by manipulating its elements. These are column, wall, slab, core, egress, and façade projects. For example, Steven Holl's Simmons Hall is used to explain a façade system that is both structural and ornamental rather than the modern model of separating the façade independently from the main structure. There are also spreads that show projects that explore three-dimensional patterns as spatial systems, such as Alfred Neumann's 1969 Synagogue. The final section shows spreads that integrate form, elements, and system as a holistic approach to architecture such as Toyo Ito's National Taichung Theater. The process is also shown through speculative projects.

Each spread is structured with a keyword, a brief description, and a visual reference such as a diagram of a project. Rather than showing a full photo of buildings, the diagrams intend to demonstrate a clear architectural intent, a way to read the project in relation to a concept.

Selection of Projects

While there is an abundance of sample projects to select from and include, we have selected projects that we find to express the Topology/Typology concepts the clearest. As we do not see Contemporary Architecture as a condition of time but as a method, the projects range in date but are predominantly from the second half of the twentieth and twenty-first century. Miguel Fisac's 1965 La Pagoda building, for example, can illustrate the plasticity and fluidity of space as three-dimensional rather than planar extrusions, a condition that UN Studio investigates in its twenty-first-century projects. The aim is to produce reference points for contemporary topics, allowing for the reference list to keep on expanding as connections are made.

The selection of projects is not meant to be understood as a ranking system or evaluation of which projects are included or omitted. Instead, it would be more relevant to interpret the selection of keywords.

27

TOPOLOGIES OF CONTAINMENT

The deformation of a topology in architecture is meant to produce a dialogue with its context by means of its relationship to the ground. Arguably, one way that architecture can be political is through its manipulation of the ground and the way a topological formation can raise it, cut it, enclose it, continue it, or extend it, producing definitions of privacy, publicness or a blurring of both through a third space.

TOPOLOGIES OF CONTAINMENT
1. Elevated
2. Courtyard
3. Quad
4. In-between
5. Piling
6. Implied Enclosure (Corners/ Points)
7. Implied Enclosure (Boundaries/ Lines)
8. Bowl
9. Interior Courtyard
10. U
11. Tunnel
12. O
13. Sky Boundary
14. Horizon
15. Layering
16. Catcher's Mitt

Fig. 50. PRAUD
The third space

137

Sample Spread

INTRODUCTION

MODERN OR CONTEMPORARY

What happens when you Google Contemporary Architecture versus
Modern Architecture? While in architecture the word "contemporary"
could relate to a building of the present time, the word "modern"
should be associated with modernism. Google's image search engine
cannot differentiate between the two and often presents the
same results or findings for either search. Searching for images
of Classical architecture or Gothic architecture produces an
output of very distinct buildings that follow a specific style.
For Contemporary Architecture, this is a problem as Modern-ism in
architecture is a distinct style. Zaha Hadid's Heydar Aliyev Center
in Baku appears on both modern, and contemporary searches, yet
this building is a project from parametricism and not modernism.

Google Image Search Engine,
2021

INTRODUCTION

FACADISM

Is this a chicken or a person?

No matter the level of detail in which this costume is designed to appear as an animal, it is evident that this is not a real chicken, but a person with a chicken mask. This applies in the same manner for understanding architecture as a relationship between its skin and bones. In "The Function of the Ornament,"[9] Moussavi and Kubo describe how the role of the architect has perhaps been limited to the design of façades in contemporary practice. This might be due to new scales of construction where the interior logic is independent of the shell or due to new performative parameters required from the façade. Designing the façade has become a specialized task.

Regardless of the envelope used for the wrapping of a building, the spatial composition takes the primary hierarchy for understanding such a building. As the colloquial phrase goes, "It's not the outside that matters, but what's on the inside that counts." For architecture, despite the level of detailed design and fabrication achieved in the façade, if the modernist Dom-ino system is still alive inside of those envelopes, then it is a modern building.

9   Moussavi, Farshid, and Michael Kubo. *The Function of Ornament*. Actar, 2008.

**Boy with Chicken Mask,
PRAUD, 2017**

INTRODUCTION

THE THIRD TYPOLOGY

"From the middle of the eighteenth century, two distinct typologies have informed the production of architecture."

"We might characterize the fundamental attribute of this third Typology as an espousal, not of an abstract nature, nor of a technological utopia, but rather of the traditional city as the locus of its concern."[10]

Such are the introductory remarks of Vidler for the description of the emerging third Typology out of the rationalist agenda, which seeks to establish a new link between the architectural form and the city. The first Typology in architecture is to be understood as the conception of elements, such as described by Laugier. The ontological form derived from these elements would emulate nature. The second Typology would focus on the mechanization of form through mass production, Typology as a system, characterized by the modernist Maison Dom-ino system. The emerging third Typology is directly linked to the production of the city through the configuration of fragments in relation to their use in the past, the boundary of the fragments, and their potential composition on a new site. Form, in this sense, is free to be deformed in a site regardless of its association to previous formal models.

---

10   Vidler, Anthony. "The Third Typology." *Theorizing a New Agenda for Architecture: An Anthology of Architectural Theory 1965-1995*, edited by Kate Nesbitt, Princeton Architectural Press, New York, NY, 1996, pp. 260-263.

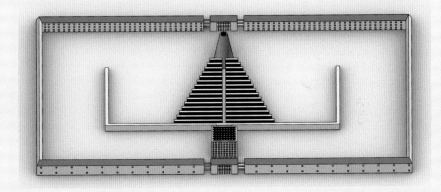

San Cataldo Cemetery,
Aldo Rossi,
Modena, Italy. 1971

INTRODUCTION

FIRST TYPOLOGY: ELEMENTS

THE PRIMITIVE HUT

Written during the time of Enlightenment, when the predominant
style was the ornamental Baroque, Abbe Laugier's "Essay on
Architecture"[11] sought to understand the basic components of what
constitutes architecture, setting aside ornamentation. Laugier
narrates the primordial relationship between man and nature
and the need for man to protect himself from nature through the
composition of a rustic cabin made from fallen branches and leaves.
This primitive hut establishes the model for the production of
any great architecture through the composition of a set of parts
consisting of columns, entablature, pediment, windows, and doors.
This abstraction of architecture reduced to a set of essential
pieces establishes the concept and foundation for understanding
architecture through its elements.

11   Laugier, Marc-Antoine, et al. *An Essay on Architecture*. Hennessey & Ingalls, 2009.

"Essai sur l'Architecture",
Marc-Antoine Laugier,
Paris, France. 1753

INTRODUCTION

TAXONOMY OF ELEMENTS

With the founding of the *École royale polytechnique* in 1794 in Paris, a new pedagogical paradigm emerged when Jean-Nicolas-Louis Durand was appointed to teach an architecture course to a group of engineering students. In 1802, Durand published the *Précis des leçons d'architecture données à l'École Polytechnique*[12] (a basic course in architecture for future engineers) where he acknowledges the difficulties of learning architecture under the current faulty methodological paradigm of teaching architecture through decoration, distribution, and construction. Instead, Durand approaches architecture from a pragmatic utilitarian perspective. His analysis of Laugier's "Primitive Hut" also points out the distinction between the use of basic architectural elements for their functionality rather than the purpose of decoration. Durand simplifies the conception of architecture to the production of building types that must be systematized through plans, sections, and elevations with an economical efficiency of form. The composition of such building types must be done through the combination and composition of architectural elements which Durand classifies as those essential for the production of space and not decoration. The *Précis,* therefore, becomes a taxonomy of building types and elements from which to choose in order to produce a building.

---

12   Durand, Jean-Nicolas-Louis. *Precis Des Lecons D'architecture Donnees a L'Ecole Polytechnique.* Hachette Livre - BNF, 2018.

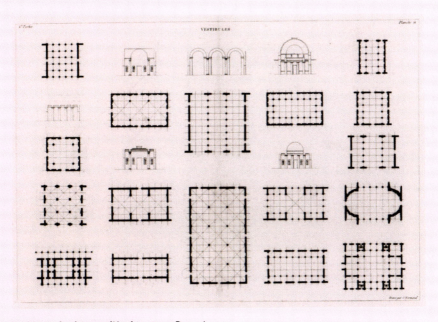

*Le Précis des leçons d'Architecture Données
à l'École Polytechnique,*
Jean-Nicolas-Louis Durand

INTRODUCTION

SECOND TYPOLOGY: SYSTEMS

DOM-INO (100 YEARS LATER)

The idea of elements as the first Typology has been ingrained into the subconscious of academia and practice, only varying by style. A wake-up call was presented during the 2014 Venice Biennale, curated by Rem Koolhaas, under the theme of "Fundamentals," which shed light on the contemporary practice focusing on a variation of these same elements.[13] In the same Biennale just outside of the main exhibition entitled "elements," a reproduction of the Maison Dom-ino was rebuilt as a wooden structure.[14] This is no coincidence because the Maison Dom-ino represents the second Typology, systems in architecture. A system has to do with the way that space is constructed, meaning varying methods of fabrication and construction produce different spaces. The rapid adoption of the Maison Dom-ino diagram as a system for rebuilding a postwar Europe became a standard for systematically building the city, a model that has been disseminated worldwide.
The reproduction of the Maison Dom-ino in a wooden system produced that criticality of presenting a different method of fabrication, which potentially could produce a different space, yet we are still building the same spatial model as the accepted standard. It questions the position of new materials and rapid prototyping fabrication methods that are façade oriented, and not spatially oriented.

13   Rethinking Windows. Part of the Fundamentals exhibition at the Venice Biennale 2014. Photo by author.
14   Maison Domino built out of wood framed structure by Valentin Bontjes van Beek and students from the Architectural Association in London for the Venice Biennale 2014 for the 100-year anniversary of the diagram. Photo by author.

Maison Dom-Ino,
Valentin Bontjes van Beek and AA students,
Venice, Italy. 2014

INTRODUCTION

THIRD TYPOLOGY: FORM

For Moneo, in his essay "On Typology,"[15] Quatremère de Quincy expressed the idea of type as the primitive feature of a building that connects it to the past. This is tied to an idea of form as type, given the example of the form of a face as primordially being round as opposed to polygonal.

> "On applique encore le mot type dans l'architecture à certaines formes générales et caractéristiques de l'édifice qui les recort."[16]
>
> De Quincy would explain the condition of a rule-based logic for understanding types as models rather than something that is explicitly copied, which he would classify as a prototype.

The photographic works of Bern and Hilla Becher document taxonomies of industrial buildings that are then arranged in a grid. From a formal perspective, the grid of water towers is not meant to be a comparative study of style but of topologies. The water towers are all different in form, but they are all still recognizable as water towers because of the inherent formal structure that a water tower must have: a heavy top to hold the water and skinny body for water pressure. This would be Quatremère de Quincy's rule based logic for water towers. Regardless of topological deformations, the root logic of the Typology must be maintained.

---

15   Moneo, Rafael. "On Typology." *A Journal for Ideas and Criticism in Architecture*, vol. 18, 1978, pp. 23–45.

16   Quincy Quatremère de. *Dictionnaire Historique D'architecture*. Librairie D'Adrien Le Clere, 1832.

41

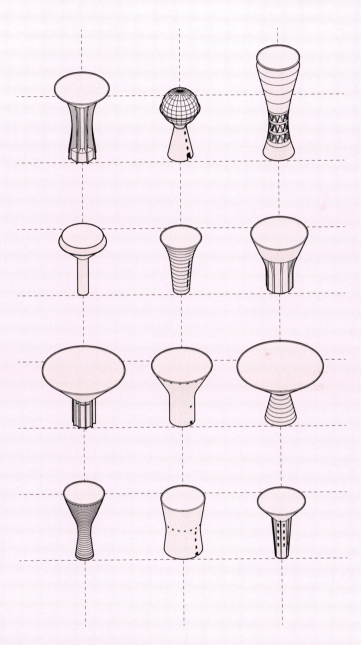

Diagram of water tower forms in reference to:
Water Towers,
Bernd and Hilla Becher,
Tate Modern, UK. 1972–2009

INTRODUCTION

"THE THIRD TYPOLOGY" Reconsidered

By Anthony Vidler

"The Third Typology" was written in 1976 as an Editorial for Oppositions 6. Revised, it was re-published two years later in Rational Architecture/Architecture Rationelle *edited by Robert Delevoy with Léon Krier Maurice Culot for the Archives d'Architecture Moderne in Brussels. Subsequently it has been anthologized and reprinted in numerous versions and languages, endowing this brief essay with a polemical authority not necessarily supported by the complexity of typological history.*[17]

But the moment in which it was written was at least auspicious. It was conceived after more than a decade of studies in Italy and elsewhere attempting to revise the functional doctrine of Modern Movement "building-types," the disastrous effects of which were manifested in postwar urban reconstruction and redevelopment. City-center after city-center had been cleared in order to create a field for the installation of more or less similar self-contained blocks, following the models laid down by CIAM between the La Sarraz Conference of 1928 and the post-war conference of 1949.

From Italy to England, criticism of modernist strategies took on different forms starting with the picturesque versions of nostalgia advanced by the Townscape movement under Gordon Cullen, moving through varieties of anthropological and sociological "Humanisms" in the breakaway groups of Team X, and finding their didactic models in versions of collage-city design proposed by Colin Rowe starting

---

17   This was in fact one of the later "typology" studies that include: "The Idea of Unity and Le Corbusier's Urban Form," *Architects' Year Book* 12. The Architectural Press, London, 1967, pp. 225-235;" A Note on the Idea of Type in Architecture," Introduction to Anne Henry, *The Building of a Club*. Cottage Club, Princeton, NJ, 1975, pp. ix-xxv; "The Third Typology," *Oppositions*, vol. 7, Winter 1976, pp. 1-4;" The Idea of Type: The Transformation of the Academic Ideal, 1750-1830," *Oppositions*, vol. 8, Spring 1977, pp. 94-115; "Type," translation and introduction to Quatremère de Quincy, *Oppositions*, vol. 8, Spring 1977, pp. 146-150; "La Troisième Typologie; The Third Typology," in *Rational Architecture*, edited by, L. Krier, M. Culot, Brussels, 1977, pp. 23-32; "On Type," *Skyline*, 1979; "A propos du type." *Archives d'Architecture Moderne*, Brussels, 1979;" Architectural Cryptograms: Style and Type in Romantic Historiography." *Perspecta*, vol. 22, 1986, pp. 136-141.

in Cambridge in 1959. Attempts were launched to revive functional typology in new guise: Sir Leslie Martin in Cambridge tried to establish the laws directing the plans and sections of science-buildings and college courts, schools, housing, offices, and university buildings derived from "better-understood functions". Sir John Summerson, the erstwhile supporter of the formalism of Soane and Dance, claimed in 1959 that the new source of the idea of unity in architecture, supplanting the traditional idea of beauty, was that of the programme.

But the idea of type referred to in "The Third Typology" was essentially counter-functionalist, at least in its "vulgar" derivatives. The group surrounding Ernesto Rogers in Casabella-Coninuità, influenced by the culturalist models of Ludovigo Quaroni and Severio Muratori, saw the building type as an integral part of city form. Carlo Aymonino and Aldo Rossi were concerned to join a morphological study of the city to the typological forms of its buildings, drawing their inspiration from urban geography and structural anthropology. The interdependence between building and city, object and context was stressed in a series of complex examples that served to undermine the crystalline purity of modernism's object-types, and to construct a vision of the city as structured fabric that allowed for both historical conservation and contemporary intervention.

The apparent "scientific" objectivity of these analyses was, however, occluded by the publication in 1962 of a short essay on type by the art-historian Giulio Carlo Argan who joined this emerging sensibility to its apparent origins in neo-classicism by a re-reading of an essay on type written in 1825 by the Perpetual Secretary of the Ecole des Beaux Arts, the antiquarian and idealist neo-classicist, Quatremère de Quincy. Quatremère's posthumous contribution to the sixties debate was an idea of typology that was not fixed by any functional determinism but rather related to a nexus or "central form" about which and to which all variations were drawn. Quatremère was, of course, speaking in Neo-Platonic terms of the Greek temple, but post-modern theorists were happy to interpret Quatremère's distinction between "model" or fixed form for copying and "type" or loose form for re-interpretation, with latitude. Joseph Rykwert, translating Argan's essay for Architectural Design, and, later, Alan Colquhoun, in a seminal essay on the formal nature of types, advanced the notion that types were in the end more formal than functional, thus permitting the re-entry into architectural discourse of a category - the "formal" - proscribed doubly by previous functionalist theories and by the more recent post '68, socio-political "advocacy" theories. It was at this stage in the discussion that "The Third Typology" was written, building on research that I had earlier published on the eighteenth-century history of the word itself, but in unabashed support for what then seemed to be the productive implications of Neo-Rationalism for an architecture that might retain its promise of modernity while retaining traces - in the abstract - of its rich, formal and socially meaningful history. The subsequent hi-jacking of typology by a crudely pictorial and static "semiology," and an regressive neo-neo-classicism, was, at that moment, not yet entirely predictable. What follows is a more detailed account of the typological discussions in Britain and the US during those years.

With the development of digital iterations of the "non-standard object" and the corresponding distancing of the discipline from its historical roots in compositional forms, the question of Typology, so actively debated in the immediate postwar period, had until recently been forgotten. With the triumph of "non-standard" permutations common to digital methods, the idea of typicality has surrendered to a combination of parametrics and historical amnesia. Architecture in the era of BIM has been left to the mercies of empiricism directed by the potential infinity of computational iterations.

This outcome was already foreshadowed in the debates of the 1960s, where typological concepts were seen as a necessary resistance to an emerging new empiricism in "design methods." This was the subject of the landmark article by Alan Colquhoun, "Typology and Design Methods," written in 1967, and stimulated by a debate with Tomás Maldonado at Princeton. Maldonado had recently retired from the Rectorship of the Hochschule für Gestaltung Ulm, where he had succeeded Max Bill, radically re-structuring what he has termed as a Bauhaus-style course toward a curriculum of scientifically directed environmental design; at Princeton he was to deliver a series of seminars that were to become his book *La Speranza progettuale: Ambiente e società* (Turin, 1971), later published in English translation as *Design, Nature, and Revolution: Toward a*

Critical Ecology (1972).[18] Colquhoun was responding to a paper circulated before the seminar, and the talk during the seminar itself. In both, Maldonado was severely criticizing the traditional design methods of existing schools and proposing a sweeping "cleaning of the Augean stables" toward a new all-encompassing discipline of environmental design.

In the circulated paper, extracts from a lecture given at the Royal College of Art the year before, Maldonado castigated the modern movement's vision of "functionalism," deplored the figure of the "architect" as a purveyor of "neo-romantic, neo-baroque, neo-expressionist formalism" producing monuments to the designer's individuality, or prophesizing "the fantastic." He criticized the untouched "ultra-conservative traditions" reigning in architectural schools of Italy and France, and others based on the foundation courses of the Bauhaus: "on the altar where Palladio was worshipped, Wright, Le Corbusier, Gropius, Mies van der Rohe, Fuller, Louis Kahn or Kenzo Tange are now being honored. The idols have been changed but not the doctrines." He concluded with a blow to history:

> Many who are worried by this state of things believe that a return to the historical study of architecture would help to define a new scientific methodology, and to surmount these shortcomings. Personally I do not believe this is the case.[19]

The Princeton seminar followed directly from this script, calling for a complete re-structuring of design education under two main headings: Physical Environmental Design and Behavioral Environmental Design, which would sweep under the separate faculties of "architecture, interior design, product design, textiles, furniture, town planning, graphic design, fashion, commercial art, glass, ceramics, silversmithing, photography, etc.,"

---

18   See Clara Isabel Neves, Joao Rocha, "The contribution of Tomas Maldonado to the scientific approach to design at the beginning of computational era. The case of HfG Ulm," in *Future Traditions. 1st cCAADe Regional International Workshop*, 2013, accessed in: papers.cumincad.org/data/works/att/ecaade2013r_002.content.pdf. Maldonado's expanded footnotes and change of title for the English edition reflected his experience of the emerging ecological movements in the US, and the debates at Princeton following his series of lectures.

19   Tomás Maldonado, "Training for the Future," Extracts from the Royal College of Art's 1965 Lethaby Lecture given in March by Dr. Maldonado, Rectore of the Hochschule für Gestaltung at Ulm," typescript, unnumbered folder, Vidler fonds, CCA p. 2.

and thus eradicate the surviving Beaux-Arts, Arts and Crafts, and Bauhaus philosophies, which considered together "constitute the most ludicrous inconsistencies ever registered in the history of education."[20]

Here the context of the Princeton lecture is important. Invited by the new Dean, Robert Geddes, on the suggestion of a young newly appointed assistant professor, Emilio Ambasz, Maldonado was the first in a series of talks dedicated to Geddes's aim to re-constitute a new School of Architecture as a school of inter-disciplinary environmental design to rival that of Berkeley. The stakes were then high, as Maldonado's audience consisted of newly appointed architects - Michael Graves, Peter Eisenman, and the invited Colquhoun - as well as historians - Kenneth Frampton and myself, all of whom were variously committed to renewing the architectural tradition, together with a roster of existing senior faculty inherited from the School of Jean Labatut. Maldonado's attack on history, and on design methods still committed to the "symbolic impositions of individual clients," by architects dreaming of the creation of "symbols of protest in cement, steel or aluminum" that "provoke no one," but result in "spectacular scenographies, to give splendour and brilliance to the tragedy (or comedy) of social stratification"[21] touched a nerve.

While Maldonado had made no reference to Typology as such, Colquhoun, fresh from the British discussion of "meaning in architecture," and corresponding typological debates in Italy, questioned the limits of empiricism and posed the need for models, related to tradition, as controls of design. He later framed the discussion thus: "Maldonado admitted that in cases where it was not possible to classify every observable activity in an architectural program, it might be necessary to use a Typology of architectural forms in order to arrive at a solution. But he added that these forms were like a cancer in the body of the solution and that as our techniques of classification became more systematic, it should be possible to eliminate them altogether."[22] Colquhoun's counter-

---

20   Tomás Maldonado, "How to Fight Complacency in Design Education," Lecture of Dr. Tomás Maldonado at the School of Architecture of Princeton University on January 5, 1966," typescript, Author's archive, unnumbered, CCA, fonds Anthony Vidler, p.5.

21   Maldonado, "Training for the Future," p. 2.

22   Alan Colquhoun, *Essays in Architectural Criticism: Modern Architecture and Historical Change*," p.43.

attack took the form of his own seminar at Princeton the following semester, which resulted in his now famous article, published as "Typology and Design Method," in the Architectural Association *Arena* a year later, an issue devoted to "Meaning in Architecture," and co-edited by George Baird and Charles Jencks.[23]

On the surface Colquhoun's argument was a straightforward defense of the need for history and tradition to control the formal decision-making left open-ended by empirical analysis. Analyzing what he considers the basis of modern architectural theory – the "bio-technical determinism" that, he argues, fails to account for a final configuration leading to a reliance on intuition that leads to an unfettered expressionism – he appeals to the psychological formulations of Ernst Gombrich. Gombrich, in *Meditations on a Hobby Horse* (a popular work among Colquhoun's circle in London), had falsified the Expressionist belief that art, rejecting all historical manifestations, communicates directly through its physiognomic and expressive content. Colquhoun drew from this the axiom that instead content is supplied by the viewer according to associations of meaning taken from lived or learned experience. In architecture this would indicate "not only that we are not free from the forms of the past, and from the availability of these forms as typological models, but that, if we assume we are free, we have lost control over a very active sector of our imagination, and of our power to communicate with others."[24]

His argument was supported by another, often cited, contemporary source, Claude-Levi-Strauss's *Structural Anthropology*, published in translation in 1963, where the anthropologist

23   Alan Colquhoun, "Typology and Design Method." *Arena*, vol. 83, June 1967, pp. 11–14. In his introduction to Colquhoun's *Collected Essays in Architectural Criticism*, Kenneth Frampton signaled "Typology and Design Method" as "seminal." [p.1] Frampton saw it as the inception of a long-standing opposition to the "various forms of reductivism" circulating in the British and European contexts of the time: "Banham's technocratic proclivities," the "cybernetic behaviourism of Christopher Alexander," and "the method-idolatry of the Hochschule für Gestaltung Ulm." Certainly, as Frampton noted, Colquhoun was an active critic of Banham's advocacy of an architecture aligned with the technological ideals of Buckminster Fuller, and, briefly, of the fantasies of Archigram, a position clearly set out in his review of Banham's *Theory and Design in the First Machine Age* of 1961. When joined with Alexander's early experiments of computational programming, and Maldonado's radical new curriculum at the HfG, Colquhoun's opposition seemed entirely aligned with his British contemporaries who sought to remain "modern" while developing a revised language for architecture that signaled some continuity with its historical tradition no matter how defined.

24   Ibid., "Typology and Design Method," p. 14.

construed societies as always inventing coherent systems of meaning, comprising what Colquhoun, via Gombrich, calls socio-spatial schemata. These are, he holds, historically, not empirically defined; Maldonado in his refusal of such typological schema, and opening empiricism to intuition, is in effect operating as aesthetically as his modern movement opponents.

As a defense of a general architectural position that saw the discipline as a continuity of continuously changing but phenomenally influential typological formulations, Colquhoun's essay was easily collected by Baird and Jencks in their *Arena* number.[25] Co-edited by George Baird and Charles Jencks, the collection was entitled "Meaning in Architecture Issue." In this issue Baird and Jencks were contesting the previous January 1967 number of *Arena*, edited by the systems theorist Francis Duffy and dedicated to problem solving – what Duffy called "determinalist functionalism" – and the measurement of the environmental effects of architecture. Duffy, in his introduction to Baird and Jencks, admitted that his issue exploring "the ways of measuring the effect that the environment of our building has upon us" had left "a number of important questions unanswered, and supported their effort to "explore the gaps."

On the surface, Colquhoun's article seemed an immediate response to this mandate. But the issue included many intimations of positions toward architectural history that would quickly contest his version: a book review by Charles Jencks of *Complexity and Contradiction in Architecture*; a consideration by the art historian Norris Kelly Smith, on "Man's Environment"; Joseph Rykwert's hermeneutic examination of "The Sitting Position – a Question of Method," which explored Quatremère de Quincy's idea that the type of the chair followed the curve of the human back (pp 15–21) and; finally, George Baird's "'La Dimension Amoureuse' in Architecture," drawing on Roland Barthes.

Indeed, Colqhoun's contribution was among the 5 original essays and 15 in the final version, the only one to use the word Typology. And while every other essay in the 1969 publication received marginal comments from other contributors, his significantly attracted none. Placed at the end of the book, "Typology and Design Method" was out-voiced, if not orphaned, by

25   Charles Jencks and George Baird, eds., *Meaning in Architecture* (London: Barrie and Rockliff, The Cresset Press, 1969).

the new proponents of semiology. Beginning with a "Glossary of Semiological Terms, and an essay on "Semiology and Architecture," by Jencks, the new version was curated as an introduction to the "nascent" theory of signs applied to architecture, and any spatial implications of Colquhoun's argument dissolved into the fragmentation of visual elements that were to emerge, in Jencks's terms, as signs of the Postmodern.

Colquhoun's silence on these developments can be explained on two fronts. First, in 1966, he was already resisting what Nikolaus Pevsner had criticized five years earlier as a "return to historicism," the emerging tendencies in architecture to stray from the modernist path of abstraction toward a series of "neo" styles. Colquhoun himself in his own practice had, following a period of Corbusian enthusiasm with the LCC housing department, developed a rigorously ascetic practice with John Miller, one that Owen Hatherley has rightly characterized as "pure" New Brutalism. Rejecting the pictorialist picturesque of Pevsner and the *Architectural Review*, he had already written a strident letter denying any picturesque influences on Le Corbusier. He equally kept a judicious distance from the historical "mannerist" associationism of Colin Rowe and his friends, including Robert Maxwell and James Stirling. He was distinctly absent from the "This is Tomorrow" group around the ICA – the Smithsons, of course, but also John McHale, the incipient "pop" theorists around Hamilton, and the social realists around Nigel Henderson.

Second, in the context of the discussions around the "meaning" of architecture Colquhoun was less influenced by the formalist tendency of English art appreciation out of Bloomsbury – Adrian Stokes as its chief spokesperson – and more attracted to the writings of the *gestalt* theorists; his essay, while it was sparked by Maldonado's reply to the question of Typology, was equally stimulated in the same semester by a lecture at Princeton by the gestalt psychologist Wolfgang Kohler. Theories of formal perception reinforced Colquhoun's conviction of the need for architectural form to communicate through its iconicity: "*the aesthetic and iconic qualities of artefacts ... [are] not so much due to an inherent property, but to a sort of availability or redundancy in them in relation to human feeling.*"[26] Examples of such redundancy in the

---

26   "Typology and Design Method." in Colquhoun, *Essays in Architectural Criticism: Modern Architecture and Historical Change*. MIT Press, Cambridge, MA, 1981, p. 48.

work of otherwise "scientific" modernists would be the space frame planning of Yona Friedman, or the demand for expression of Yannis Xenakis' Philip's pavilion.

This conclusion points to Colquhoun's solution: in order to avoid an unthinking "reversion" to tradition, and any idea of "a fixed and immutable relation between forms and meaning," he proposes, for a period of constant change investigating "the part which modifications of type-solutions play in relation to problems and solutions which are without precedent in any received tradition." His solution: "Not a process of reduction" but "rather process of exclusion." He gives the example (significantly enough not in architecture) but in art and music of Kandinsky and Schoenberg. Where "traditional formal devices were not completely abandoned but were transformed and given new emphasis by *the exclusion of ideologically repulsive elements*" [my italics], Colquhoun invests this process of exclusion with the value of encouraging a kind of seeing innocently, "enabling us to see the potentiality of forms as if for the first time and with naiveté."[27]

In a presentation of their "Recent Work" at the AA in 1976, Colquhoun and Miller described their practice with a series of axonometrics and plans, with black and white photos, demonstrating the careful assessment of the brief, the site, and the modulation of spaces demanded by the program, all composed within groupings and clusters unified in an overall parti. The origin of this "parti" is ascribed to no "historical" precedent, but to a kind of logic of assemblage guided by the logic of the constructional system employed. The distance from the Smithsons could not have been more evident. There was no rhetoric of "as found," no rhetoric of material, as in the Hunstanton School, no rhetoric of the topological plan as in the Sheffield University competition, not even the neo-Palladian rhetoric of the Liverpool Cathedral project. Indeed, if there is a rhetoric at all, it's one of severe reduction to the surfaces of enclosure – not as abstract aesthetic formulations.

At the end of this presentation, Colquhoun took questions from two of the audience. Kenneth Frampton, from his recent reading of Arent, asks not about the aesthetics, but about the relations between public and private – what he called the honorary spatial development demanded by the public role of the buildings – i.e. the

27   Ibid., p. 50.

entrance to the Activity Center. Colquhoun admitted that this might have been more considered.

The second and repeated question came from Leon Krier who remarked that as far as he was concerned all the buildings "looked the same" and could have, for that matter, been the same – any of them could have been any function, all were equally indeterminate; none exhibited the character of their use. Colquhoun vehemently (or as mildly vehemently as he was able) repudiated any idea of designing a building to look like it was – this would be to create, as, per Venturi, a "Duck." The idea of character was "not a necessary proposition for architecture," he stated; the "inherent expression of the inner nature of a building was impossible" to effect. And anyway, many of his projects had been designed precisely for multiple different uses over time.

Here the vocabulary of type, whether the already formulated types of the modern movement (the Unité, for example) and the re-cycled type forms of the so-called rationalist Enlightenment, was to be excluded; the public realm demanded a restrained rhetoric, one that could hardly be recognized except through continuous experience of use and the *gestalt* of the particular building – a school that because of new social and educational conditions was like no previous school, but became recognized as a school through occupational and visual understanding.

When this proposition is examined at a distance, it is clear that what guided Colquhoun as a mental model for alteration, extrapolation, and re-formulation was one derived from the academic tradition so criticized by Banham – compositional organizations, distributed along axes and arranged according to scales of spaces, but now devoid of the "rules" championed by the Beaux-Arts, and not yet controlled by the historical nostalgia of the Rowe/Venturi complex. As Colquhoun stated in his AA School presentation, "The architectural problem presents itself as the need to satisfy the demands of distribution, environment, site, construction, etc., but the designer would be unable to decide on a distributive scheme unless he already had a certain ideal configuration in his mind. This is the constant against which possible solutions are measured. The design process would seem to be more dialectical than deductive."

In this sense, Colquhoun's use of the word Typology referred more to his own abstract understanding of the role of history in architecture – rather than drawn from a debate that had only recently developed in the Italian context and was imported to London by Joseph Rykwert. Published in *Architectural Design*, in December 1963, Rykwert's translation of an article by Giulio Carlo Argan, "On the Typology of Architecture" ("Sul concetto di tipologia architecttonica"), had introduced ideas that were circulating in Rome and Venice from the late 1950s. Introducing his translation, Rykwert noted that Argan's article had first appeared in Italian in 1962 and that "it seemed to the translator to approach a subject which is central to architectural theory both in this country and in America – but to do so from a rather unfamiliar standpoint and to contribute a new element to current discussion," elements that as Argan noted had been developed by Sergio Bettini in the international journal *Lotus* in 1961, and which in more general terms had developed around Venice School of Architecture under the leadership of Saverio Muratori.[28] Thus, by the time of the debate between Colquhoun and Maldonado, these interventions were well-known throughout Europe and certainly followed in Britain, and had been supported by the publications of Aymonino and Rossi as they inherited the courses in composition from Muratori.

Rossi's developed theory of type, sketched in a series of programs and memoranda to his students in Venice and Zurich, was adumbrated in the collection of essays comprising *Architettura e la città* of 1966. Here he departed from the visual aspects of the city, to understand the city *as* architecture – "as construction, the construction of the city over time" – according to the fundamental aesthetic and social intents of its builders. His "typology" was construed along the lines of the division introduced by Quatremère de Quincy in the 1820s, that between the fixed forms of a "model" and more general and open relations of elements forming the "type." For Rossi the type subsumed the ordinary meaning of function, and was irreducible to a single semiotic element: it was holistic, at once spatial and social, and embedded in the fabric of the city, which was, in turn, its history.

The Third Typology Redux

In "The Third Typology" I distinguished two ways in which modern theorists since the eighteenth-century Enlightenment had sought

28   For a detailed account of Muratori's typological theories, see Giancarlo Cataldi, Gian Luigi Maffei and Paolo Vaccaro, "Saverio Muratori and the Italian School of Planning Typology." *Urban Morphology*, vol. 6, no.1, 2002, pp. 3-14.

to classify the elements and forms of buildings, three concepts by which the authority of design might be established. The first was the structural model of Laugier: the infamous primitive hut, before which all subsequent buildings had to be measured. The three elements of a building – column, beam, and roof member - prefigured in a Rousseauesque vision of the first shelter were for Laugier the instruments of purification, the arbiters of architectural language. This was a Typology, a knowledge of type founded on an idea of rational nature.

The second Typology, emerging in the nineteenth-century, stressed the analogy of a building to a machine, a functional comparison that proposed a fit between form and function as close as that existing between the forms of a steam engine and its performance requirements. Bentham's Panopticon was a good, if extreme, example of this, a sensibility that was to be re-interpreted in modernism – the house as a machine for living in, etc. This was a Typology based not on nature but on that new nature created by industrial production as, since the first industrial revolution, a humanistically conceived architecture has been forced to assimilate the emerging realities of machine production. Its claim was to constitute new institutional forms, organically and productively, from the hospital to the prison, that would both serve and order the new bourgeois city. Michel Foucault, also writing in the late sixties, had dramatically pointed to the hidden structures of power embodied in these modern institutions, characterizing their discourse by reference to the Panopticon of Jeremy Bentham, that building invented like a machine to order the lives and perceptions if not reform the souls of criminals incarcerated therein.

The problem of this machine analogy for architecture, however, resided not so much in its application to institutional forms, but rather to the major problem of mass society itself, the attempted solution of the housing question. The conflation of the problem of a "machine architecture" with that of housing, under the guise of "mass housing," was in the twenties one of the watchwords of modernism's socio-architectural program; in its postwar versions, it has become the object of severe criticism as Martin Pawley's *Architecture versus Housing* reminded us.

This double problem was construed in two ways, sometimes conflated; the Benthamite image of the economically functioning machine was adduced by architects to explain how architecture might better serve a society on which it was dependent, or even operate on that society for its reform or control in the manner of a technical instrument. The idea of architecture as an "engine" for the modification of human behavior and the notion of its institutional character easily led to the postulation of the communal dwelling, from Fourier's Phalanstery to Godin's Familistery and finally to Le Corbusier's own Unité d'habitation. A second effect of industrialization, however, was, of course, to supply mass-produced standardized parts for the assembly of utilitarian buildings: the glasshouses, railway sheds, and exhibition halls, of which the Crystal Palace was the most paradigmatic example. Such constructions were hardly admitted into "architecture" at first, by virtue of their unabashedly temporary and serial qualities. The machine was thus absorbed by architecture in two ways: architecture could function like a machine and gain a new identity for itself aesthetically and programmatically through analogy; or it could actually be produced by machine and derive its new forms from the world of industrial processes.

In the nineteenth-century, both modes of relating to the machine were retained within a traditional conception of architecture by being subordinated to the idea of type. The type "prison" or the type "exhibition hall," although developed to serve new social needs, were each understood to partake of the architectural tradition by their formal reference to traditional typologies. The central plan of the Panopticon turned the vision of Renaissance order upon itself; the "cathedral" form of the Crystal Palace endowed the profane with sacred authority. Some types, like hospitals, were built up of typical elements (ward-blocks) and relied on the grid of the classical town to give them institutional form. The "type" of the commune, as I have mentioned, quickly adopted the old type "palace" in order to constitute "people's palaces."

With the introduction of the need for mass housing, however, this interrelation of machine analogy and traditional type-form began to break down. The initial assimilation to the type "palace" (the Phalanstery of Fourier, the Familistery of Godin) was rapidly overtaken by the expanding demand for quickly constructed and cheap dwellings. The "architectural" boundaries of the problem were overrun, and housing became more an affair of

> economics and politics to be controlled, if at all, by
> the techniques of zoning.

The modern movement attempted to overcome this problem on behalf of architecture by formulating new typologies for housing and their technical systems of construction. The most sophisticated version of this attempt was produced by Le Corbusier. He proposed an acceptance of the machine at the level of both analogy and production: the iconography of the Villa at Garches referred to the idea of a "machine for living in" and the specifications of the Maison Citrohan transferred the mass-production techniques of Ford, analogically at least, to those of houses. Gropius, similarly, despite his professed craft affiliations, or perhaps because of the alliance of the Arts and Crafts movement to popular, rather than high culture, in the end thought of housing as the rational aggregation of units according to scientific criteria of planning, orientation, amenity, and construction. The extruded section of the *siedlung* row house succeeds in eliminating any traditional idea of formal or harmonic unity. While Le Corbusier eradicated the dichotomy between "Architecture" and "Building" by raising all tasks to the status of an aesthetically governed architecture, the theoreticians of the *neue sachlichkeit* tended to reduce all to a single level of building in the name of rational function.

In its implications for urbanism, if not for architecture, the result was the same. The common emphasis on type was an evident attempt once more to make out of housing an institutional form, susceptible to the ordering devices of the architect. Herein lay the critical failure of the modern movement in the domain of housing; for when these "institutions," however carefully devised and technically realized, were replicated *en masse*, their hermetic and self-contained forms proved antipathetical to any vision of urban and ultimately social continuity and connectivity. When allied to the pathology of the nineteenth-century slum, which called for sun, light, air, and greenery, these types destroyed the urban street and denied the urban culture of their intended inhabitants. The critique of this modern movement tradition has occupied architects and planners since the 1950s, from Team X to the Neo-Rationalists; but the contradictions still largely remain, between a tradition of formal design that stresses unity and understanding of the city that embraces both its potential insalubrity and its culture, a mass market society expanding into ever-multiplied consumer markets, and a mass-production potential that has yet to be completely realized within the building industry.

I had, in the 1970s, already written the history of this tendency toward the institutional formalization of a housing problem that I saw as more intimately linked to the form of cities, and especially the nature of their streets. In a study of the ideal "architectural" street from the Enlightenment to the end of the nineteenth century, posed against the "real" historical street, I pointed to the relentless war waged by architecture and urbanism against the city, that ended in the triumph, in architectural ideology, of the anti-street model. Accordingly, against the Corbusian hatred of the Balzacian street, I posed a sensibility toward the street as a historical and cultural condenser and signifier, the only form of city life that acted to counter the dismembering of social and political life by the processes of suburbanization, gentrification, and urban renewal. Hence the idea behind the third Typology.

To the first two typologies then, following Rossi, I added a third, post-modernist Typology, where the former two were absorbed within the framework of the city as a whole. In this notion the city became the generator of forms that were so integrally connected to their functions in daily life that, even if these forms took on a life of their own, they would retain some sense, some levels of meaning, from their functioning past. This was a Typology based on history and on the urban structure conceived of as a virtually generating force; one that allowed for the introduction of memory and temporal reference into a hitherto timeless vision of type.

> With the current reappraisal of the idea of progress, and with this, the critique of the Modern Movement ideology of productivism, architects have turned to a vision of the primal past of architecture - its own constructive and formal bases as evinced in the preindustrial city. Once again the issue of typology is raised in architecture, not this time with a need to search outside the practice for legitimation in science or technology, but with a sense that within architecture itself resides a unique and particular mode of production and explanation. From Aldo Rossi's transformations of the formal structure and institutional types of eighteenth-century urbanism,

to the sketches of the brother's Krier that recall
the "primitive" types of shelter imagined by the
eighteenth century philosophes, rapidly multiplying
examples suggest the emergence of a new, third
typology.

I characterized the fundamental attribute of this third Typology
as an espousal, not of an abstract nature, nor of a technological
utopia, but rather of the city. The city, I argued, following Rossi,
provided the material for classification and the forms of its
artifacts over time provided the basis for re-composition. I
acknowledged that this third Typology, like the first two, was
clearly based on reason, classification, and a sense of the public
in architecture; but I held that, unlike the first two, however, it
proposed no absolute panacea, no ultimate apotheosis of man in
architecture, no positivistic methodology. In its adherence to
rationalism as a guiding principle, it differed markedly from the
latter-day romanticisms of "townscape," "strip city," and "collage
city" that had been proposed as replacements for modern movement
urbanism since the fifties. The fundamental characteristic of
this manner was its self-referentiality. Where, in the first two
typologies architecture, made by man, was being compared and
legitimized by another "nature" outside itself, in the third, as
exemplified by the work of the Neo-Rationalists, there was no such
attempt at validation. Columns, houses, and urban spaces seemed
to refer only to their own nature as architectural elements; their
geometries seemed less scientific or technical than essentially
architectural. I proposed that Rossi and his colleagues were
opposing the "cultural" nature of the city, to the scientific nature
of nature.

This concept of the city as the site of a new
typology is evidently born of a desire to stress
the continuity of form and history against
the fragmentation produced by the elemental,
institutional and mechanistic typologies of the
recent past. The city is considered as a whole, its
past and present revealed in its physical structure…

I then analyzed what I felt to be the formal procedures of this
Typology, one drawn from the deep structural nature of a city grown
up over time. I showed how elements were selected and reassembled
according to criteria derived from three levels of meaning: the

first, inherited from meanings ascribed by the past existence of the forms; the second, derived from choice of the specific fragment and its boundaries, which often cross between previous types; the third, proposed by a re-composition of these fragments in a new context.

The crux of my argument, and in the event its most fallible part, related to *meaning*, is that elusive chimera of postmodern architecture. I tried to demonstrate that.

> When a series of typical forms is selected from the past of a city, they do not come, however dismembered, deprived of their original political and social meaning. The original sense of the form, the layers of accrued implication deposited by time and human experience cannot be lightly brushed away; and certainly, it is not the intention of the Neo-Rationalists to disinfect their types in this way. Rather, the carried meanings of these types may be used to provide a key to their newly invested meanings. The technique, or rather the fundamental compositional method suggested by the Neo-Rationalists, is the transformation of selected types – partial or whole – into entirely new entities that draw their communicative power and potential critical force from the understanding of this transformation.

My example of this "sticky meaning" theory was the City Hall project for Trieste, by Aldo Rossi. Critics had referred to it as an evocation of a late eighteenth-century prison, and I advanced the theory that Rossi had in fact cunningly used this theme to give new meaning to his own project. Tafuri had after all shown that in the period of the first formalization of the prison type, as Piranesi demonstrated, it was possible to see in "prison" a powerfully comprehensive image of the dilemma of society itself poised between a disintegrating religious faith and a materialist reason. Now, Rossi, in ascribing to the city-hall (itself a recognizable nineteenth-century type) the affect of prison, achieved a new level of signification, which evidently referred to the ambiguous condition of city government. In the formulation, the two types were not merged: indeed, "city-hall" had been replaced by an open arcade standing in contradiction on a prison base, itself a clear reference to Boullée's Palace of Justice. In this visionary image, well-known to Rossi who had published the first translation of Boullée into Italian, Boullée had placed the abstract cube of the palace on top of the rusticated base that served as a subterranean prison; he spoke of justice trampling crime underfoot, an image reinforced by the architectural contrast. I concluded, somewhat polemically,

> The dialectic is clear: the society that understands the reference to the prison will still have need of the reminder, while at the very point that the image finally loses all meaning, the society will either have become entirely "prison," or, perhaps, its opposite.

Then, expanding the definition of the new Typology to include the work of Leon Krier and the Neo-Rationalists in general, I pointed to its explicit criticism of the modern movement as it utilizes the images of urban order derived from the preindustrial city to bind up the fragmentation, decentralization, and formal disintegration introduced into contemporary urban life by the zoning techniques and technological advances of the twenties.

> While the Modern Movement found its hell in the closed, cramped, and insalubrious quarters of the old industrial cities, and its Eden in the uninterrupted sea of sunlit space filled with greenery – a city become a garden – the new typology as a critique of modern urbanism raises the continuous fabric, the clear distinction between public and private marked by the walls of street and square to the level of principle. Its nightmare is the isolated building set in an undifferentiated park.

This somewhat naively hopeful "third typology" has been deservedly subjected to much criticism, from both the political point of view – how might we calibrate the political power of what in the end is reduced to the rhetorical gesture of historical reference in form? – and the formal point of view – how might we draw the line between a fertile and authentic absorption of historical reference in architecture and a proliferation of quotations that reduce themselves to kitsch? My "third typology" neither addressed these questions nor indicated any means of defense against the worst a-political quotation mongering of a post-modernism too quickly consumed.

Perhaps, in the first place, one might ascribe this to the over-caricatured "history" of the three typologies themselves, and notably that of the second. Certainly, in the over-mechanistic formulation of the second, modernist Typology, I severely understated the commitment of many modernists, especially Le Corbusier, to historical continuity and formal allusion, not so much in his urbanism, but in his architecture. In this way, I fell into the trap of creating as much of a "paper tiger" of an oversimplified and all-embracing devil "modernism" as that of the postmodernists I thought I was staunchly attacking.

Thus, to take only the case of Le Corbusier, characterized in "The Third Typology" as a pure exponent of the machinist sensibility. Of course he was, but he was also, as I in fact knew very well, a historicist traditionalist, in his own fashion. Despite his ideological and iconographic appeal to the twin heroes of modern technocracy, F.W. Taylor and Henry Ford, Le Corbusier retained a profoundly traditional vision of architecture. Each house, each villa, was endowed with a specific and humanistically idealized geometry; its masses, surface, proportions, and spatial organization were all subjected to the canons of a purist classicism. Thus, the Palladian type offers a paradigm for the Villa at Garches, as Colin Rowe has demonstrated, while the artist's studio presents a vision of "elevated" living for the masses. The Saint-Simonian, technocracy living in the machinist villa, the Weberian democracy living in lofts that by implication/association endow them with the artistic charisma so sadly lacking in their daily life. From the villa, with its roots in Palladian prototypes, to the mass-produced house, with its references to the artist's studio type, there existed an unbreakable chain. Similarly, when the single units of dwelling were aggregated, a new scale of type-form was proposed: the historical continuity provided by the monks' cells at the Chartreuse of Ema, modernized in the apartments of the Immeubles villas, the horizontal Phalanstery in the vertical Unité d'habitation, each subsuming their mass-produced elements in a complete whole, a new type of architectural unity.

In *Vers une Architecture*, accordingly, Le Corbusier looked at history on two levels: that of the "essence" of architecture, the constituents, as it were of the eternally architectural, and that of the tradition of designed architecture - the codes and motifs of the profession. On the one hand, there was the formal analysis of masses, surfaces, and solids and voids revealed in light - the drawings of the Pompeian courtyards are exemplary of this - and which offer a primer into the "origins" of the art. On the other hand, there are the type forms and already developed solutions to typical social functions, from the villa to the house, that have been worked out in the classical tradition [eternal architecture versus coded professional architecture - a new version of the absolute (natural) and the arbitrary (customary)]. On the one hand, the play of essences, the true return to origins, characteristic of eighteenth-century Enlightenment - the origins of sensibility toward the play of light on surface, or the emergence of almost natural types, uncodified, inchoate, elemental, brutal. On the other, the careful, often witty inversion of already codified architecture; the discourse on the professional humanist tradition; a re-formulation of codified types of architecture - from Michelangelo's Saint Peter's to Palladios villas.

The parallel drawn by Colin Rowe, between the villa type of Palladio and that of Le Corbusier, as demonstrated by careful geometrical proof, represents more than a passing affiliation. Adopting the alternating bay rhythms of Palladio, Corbusier deliberately reverses, turns inside out, and deforms the original structure of the type to develop, with an intensity rarely attained since, a new formulation. This new "villa" relying for its modern cultural meaning on the reference to its traditional counterpart, establishing its new semantics on the basis of inversions and displacements of the old, stands not so much as a rupture with the past as a careful deconstruction of a classical tradition become academic, a renewing of its possibilities for invention and production. Here Le Corbusier was operating in the manner of a true formalist: the creation of a new lexicon was impossible without the calculated explosion of the old. In the case of Garches, one might go further on the lines suggested by Rowe, to propose that with the renewal of signs, the retention of a fundamental syntax and grammar was essential to any new meaning. That Le Corbusier consciously chose the Palladian villa as his type of architectural grammar indicates the force of the original form in carrying, over three centuries and often by the deployment of the slightest reference, the message of the presence of humanism. It could be utilized as "grammar" only because its own organization, identified so precisely by Wittkower, had become so quickly a "sign" of the classical, of architecture itself. If there had been time, in the limits of the polemical essay, to elaborate such an analysis, perhaps the question of abstraction and history might have been addressed in the third Typology, allowing in turn for a less simplistic reading of Rossi's typological manipulations.

Second, in referring again somewhat simplistically to the "history" of the city, and its structural nature, I was in fact falling into an idealization commonly held by anthropologists, archaeologists, and some historians since the late nineteenth-century one indeed seized on by Rossi himself in *The Architecture of the City*. In this book Rossi referred to the work of Foustel de Coulanges, whose writing on the antique city in the 1860s had attempted to trace the structural relationships between classes, economics, and culture in the ancient world, almost as if historical change had, for a moment, been suspended. Rossi was similarly attracted to the writings of Claude Levi-Strauss, the structural anthropologist, who spoke of the eternal fabric, the timeless textures of the city. Such a city would indeed offer itself up to just the kind of formal manipulation I had described in the Trieste project, one that, precisely because time was suspended, automatically captured the meaning of all times. Such a vision of history was, of course, entirely opposed to my parallel argument about the essentially political and critical nature of the third Typology, its dialectical relationship to the present.

63

TOPO

Index Part 1

OLOGY

While traditional methods of representing architecture have relied on planimetric projections, a mathematical conception of space as topological has transitioned architecture in the twenty-first century as a formal operation. This has generated several polemics and debates on the issues and roles of form in architecture, such as the long battle between form and function. This section discusses these issues making the case for form working as a system for making space regardless of function. Space is inherently useful. When a human is presented with free space, it will find a use for it. If we re-examine Laugier's exercise of imagining a man in his first origin, in the process of finding shelter, we should reconsider the cave again instead of rapidly dismissing it. The cave is a pure form, autonomous to any design authority, and fabricated parametrically through the forces of time and nature. "A cave presents itself to his view, he slides into it, and finding himself dry applauds his discovery." In Laugier's hypothetical, the man moves on to experimenting with branches due to his lack of control of the light and air quality in the cave, and builds the Primitive Hut. Yet, the cave had issues that could be fixed technically, making the cave more comfortable today (perhaps by adding electrical systems, HVAC, some plumbing, and a door?).[1] If form is presented, humans will find a way to adopt it, and use it. Form may be manipulated (deformed) with a specific purpose and intent of functionality, or randomly found as the cave. The following spreads present these and other issues on form.

1 Look at ENSAMBLE STUDIO's Truffle House, an experiment on prefabricated forms. "The Truffle: Ensamble-Studio." Ensamble, https://www.ensamble.info/thetruffle.

Did Technology Kill the Box?

Interview with Ben van Berkel

PRAUD   When looking at your overall body of work, the theme of fluid space and movement evolves in parallel to advancements in modeling software, construction technology and material science. These are aspects that your firm has been able to research deeply and rigorously, generating a transition from curved walls in a Euclidean plane, as seen in the Villa Wilbrink (1992), to the topological investigations in your current work where space is no longer Euclidean but three-dimensional.
Would you say that the manipulation of form in your projects has been directly impacted by the technological capacity of the time? Or is it the other way around, has it been the understanding of the topological deformations that has pushed the technology, led by your own research not found in the general construction industry?

BvB   We are interested in how technology can generate the unexpected in form-making. But I have also always been interested in systems of control, and how you can direct technology in the search for form-making and bring that into construction in order to develop it further. You are indeed correct in saying that we have had a long-term interest in topological deformations. These are often found in how topological surfaces can direct how you organise space.

PRAUD   An example of this condition can be seen in the transition of form in two similar typologies: residential with the Möbius House (1993) and Villa NM (2000); and Theatre with the Theatre Agora (2002-2007) and the Theatre de Stoep (2008-2014). In the residential projects, the form for both projects could be explained diagrammatically in a similar methodology using the wireframe of boxes. Yet, in the final execution, the Möbius House represents the formal contortions of the box achieving the Möbius House, while Villa NM achieves the deformations via the lofting of surfaces.

These could be interpreted directly to changes in software technology, but is this really the case or were there different formal agendas that you were investigating?
The reason I ask is because when comparing the theatres (Agora and de Stoep) a similar condition happens where the formal diagrams can always be abstracted to the box wireframe, yet the execution is performed one through planes (Agora) and one through lofting (de Stoep). Could you elaborate on these conditions?

BvB   We did a great deal of study into topological surfaces, but we also learnt from the history of how they have previously been used in combined ways within engineering and architecture. Frei Otto's bubble experiments and diagrams were also extremely influential to our research into how loads can be carried through a single-edge surface. You mention the Theatre Agora and Theatre de Stoep, but I would in fact say that the Music Theatre we designed in Graz perhaps illustrates our investigations more fully. There, we used a strategy where a Seifert surface originated from a box wire frame principle, so the project was executed through a richer plane structure, as topological surfaces and Seifert surfaces combined different efficiencies. Many surfaces can interact with the Seifert surface. This is something we also applied in the transfer terminal of Arnhem Central Station. There, the Seifert surface enables the support of huge cantilevers, but it was also used to create specific viewpoints for guided orientation and flows through the station. It enabled the architecture to guide movement, creating a kind of natural wayfinding and lessening for need for signage. With these projects we also learnt that while you may start with a certain set of geometric principles, these may change along the way due to external forces or internal regulations, such as materiality. For instance, in the Music Theatre in Graz, we realised that we had to pump the concrete into the molds from below, rather than pouring it from above, and in Arnhem Central Station, although the twisting central column was originally designed to be built in concrete, it was eventually made with steel, which required the use of ship-building techniques. This change meant that although the surfaces were much thinner, they could carry more weight. Another essential approach was to be reductive, but use repetition. This we did with the 3 angles used in the Möbius house, for example. Here, angles of 7, 9, and 11 degrees were repeated throughout the house, which in turn created a kind of natural rhythm in how you experience moving through the home. Perhaps this could be likened to a serial composition by Philip Glass, where simplicity, reduction, and repetition create a kind of meditative rhythm.

PRAUD   Lastly, we see in a period of four years, a series of pavilions (Holiday Home in 2006, The Changing Room in 2008, New Amsterdam Plein and pavilion in 2008, Burnham Pavilion in 2009, Youturn Pavilion in 2010) demonstrate the merger of elements and system to produce a holistic space. What I mean by holistic is, that unlike modernism where you have elements (stairs, columns, slab, walls) following a Dom-ino system, your pavilions produce a spatial effect, ornamentation, structure, enclosure, and form through the use of one element that performs in all these capacities.
One of my favorites is the Burnham Pavilion. Was it meant to reference Mies van der Rohe's Farnsworth House? What was the intention?

BvB   I see it as a nod to, or a celebration of the modernist model, but it also very much represents the contemporary condition in which we find ourselves now. As you say, rather than using separate elements, both the space and your experience of it become continuous. In the Burnham Pavilion, the roof guides the void spaces and turns them into columns. They then act as "Big Details" that integrate different qualities. The pavilion references Burnham's plan of Chicago, with its network of diagonal streets, while simultaneously opening up (vertical) diagonal views of the city and the skyscrapers that overlook the park. It literally offers a different perspective.

PRAUD   I would like to read this project (The Burnham Pavilion) as a direct reference to the Farnsworth House, and a break in the modernist canon, replaced by a multi-performative fluid element. Yet, unlike the other pavilions that stand as singular formal objects, the Burnham Pavilion is not really formal;

instead it displays a system of space, a new diagram replacing the Dom-ino diagram. Would you read it in the same manner? Would you say that the notion of producing fluid space is a singular formal intention or could it be systematic as the Dom-ino was for modernism? Are spatial systems also something that is being studied at UNSense?

BvB   In the Netherlands in the 1920s and 1930s we also had a movement called the "Nieuwe Zakelijkheid" (New Objectivity or New Pragmatism) which worked with concepts similar to that of the Dom-ino. But I wouldn't describe the fluid space as a singular formal intention as such, nor as systematic, in the Dom-ino sense. It contains a double ambition: to improve the spatial experience while making these complex experiences more modular. An example of this is the Mercedes-Benz Museum in Stuttgart. There we wanted to investigate how you could go beyond the modernist, perspectival space – where the space is always in front of you and you view it as if through a camera – and instead create a kind of kaleidoscopic experience, where it is as if the space follows you. But you also have to convince the parties that are involved in construction that you have a buildable system. So again, a reductive and repeated element is introduced, in this case, the recurring element of the "twist" (see diagram below). This repetition creates a complex, flower-like reading of the building. This was an approach that also led us to the development of what we call "Design Models," new forms of modularity that can be understood to be formal, whilst also affecting how we experience space. This concept of repetition was also applied in the branding manual strategy we adopted for the stations on the new Doha Metro Network. The Burnham Pavilion also plays with this double approach to spatial experience and repetition, but I don't see it as simply a practical, modular approach like the Dom-ino. I see it as an inclusive strategy; a "Big Detail" that primarily determines how the building is experienced.

***

On Topology

Interview with Greg Lynn

PRAUD   We are interested in knowing how your views on
Topology and form have changed since you first introduced the
Animate Form more than two decades ago. The book was published
in 1999, but your studies have been well documented from earlier
lectures at the AA, and GSD, where the recurring topics of
discussion were the Virtual versus the Actual, differential calculus
and the curve, The Objectile from Bernard Cache, and symmetry as a
mutation from the lack of information from William Bateson.

GL   I was never that interested in Topology as a concept,
        merely as a geometric and formal process that provided
        an alternative to composition with primitive solids; for
        example the "Objects-types" articulated by Corbusier
        in his publication Vers une architecture. I found the
        persistence of the use of primitive solids troubling
        even in the work of contemporary architects like those
        included in the Deconstructivist Architecture show,
        as even though they deformed and tortured geometries
        they still relied on indexing these results back to
        primitive forms. For me, Topology was a handy geometric
        medium to redefine what a conceptual primitive could be.
        There was a great upheaval in the sciences in the 1980s
        and 1990s rethinking simple variation and deformation
        (gradients of differences) and engaging concepts like
        those introduced by William Bateson in the late 1800s
        to describe that with variation in nature there was not
        infinite gradiation but in fact simplification. This
        simplification is not reducible to analysis back to
        types but to complex homeostatic processes built into
        simple mathematical, chemical and biological models. With
        the availability of massively powerful computation on
        desktops 40 years ago when I was starting as a designer
        it was possible to formulate an alternative to "Object

type" on thinking about an architectural primitive, one based on transformation through deformation, to concepts of unfolding of simple rules as a method of variation. Like many at the time I was inspired by the modelling of complex forms and behaviors through the use of simple mathematical algorithms at places like the Santa Fe Institute. Many of the lectures and symposia you mentioned included their members who were very curious about how architects were using computation. The use of simple algorithms to produce something built from many complex parts like a building was attractive to them. Sadly, mostly what they observed were manual deformations using digital tools and not generative processes. One would have to say for the last 40 years this has been a failed experiment to some degree and a success in other ways. The preponderance of tools being used for generating design details and rationalizing construction is amazing. The conceptual engagement with this as primarily a stylistic event is disappointing.

PRAUD   Form and the Virtual: The "internet of things" has evolved now as an actual space of interaction that has shifted to the "Internet of Value." There are whole economies and exchanges happening in this space that have almost surpassed being a heterotopia of the actual.
The use of Hololens, for example, can be used as a tool of design and construction, but it can also augment the actual reality, where what one experiences is a manifestation of the representational.
We don't foresee everyone wearing hololenses on a daily basis to navigate the streets, but we would say this fusion is not farfetched through some sort of Google contact lenses as Michio Kaku discusses. Going back to the *Animate Form*, one could experience topological transformations, and deformations in real time as a continuous animation of space.
What is the role of form nowadays when the representational or virtual has become the actual? I would describe The Atlantis Sentosa Resort as dealing with this dynamic.

GL   I agree that the expectations for the built environment remain modest by most people and it has always been the case. People are comfortable with the familiar and stimulated by the new. It might very well be that what we call the "built environment" meaning buildings are expected to be comforting while what we call "entertainment, technology, communication, and media" is expected to be stimulating. McLuhan distinguished technologies as hot and cold but it could be related to physicality and occupation that some things are hot and others cold. Regardless, architects are primarily in the comfort business and at best produce environments that are "cool." What Frank, Peter and I were trying to do with Sentosa Island was something that wasn't comforting and wasn't cool. We aligned the spatial and formal environment with technology and media at a vast scale as a proposition. We also used technology in the design process in a very intensive way. For both myself and Frank it was an intense immersion in design media and technology at the earliest stages of design and this has to be related to the follow through of technology and its integration into the spatial experiences we were designing. This is different than the "decorated shed" in the sense that decoration is assumed to come later and be additive. We were thinking of media as original in the earliest stages of the design concept.

PRAUD   The Objectile and Robotics: We really enjoyed the definition of the Objectile you presented by Bernard Cache and your earlier focus on Topology as a manifestation of force and motion. Topologies didn't need to move themselves to describe movement. Topologies could be said to represent a single frame in a sequence of a deformation process, as was the case for the OMV H2 House in 1996.
This view shifted a bit more into robotics and the possibility of not only embedding forces into the form but having the form move itself, as in the London Olympic Dome (2009) or the RV Prototype (2012).
As robotics, AI, machine learning, and deep learning become more advanced, how is this impacting your proposals on Form as a moving responsive entity?

GL   Bernard was not only the person who introduced CNC manufacturing to an audience of architects, designers and theorists first, he was also designing purely through algorithms. Karl Chu was another who was 100% devoted to designing using algorithms. These were very bold and powerful propositions. Now while almost everyone is using scripts in their design processes, the scripts are often quite banal. Bernard and Karl's were anything but banal. They also were not interested in "experiments" and "happy accidents" they were designing algorithms with specific intent. I was never as hard core as either Karl or Bernard and have always compromised in favor of expedience and control over design in a conventional sense. But I will never write a code from which a collection of buildings unfold. Bernard's term "objectile" is defining a simple concept that unfolds, very similar to Bateson's concept of genetic unfolding. The Embryological House was done by drawing six compatible curves that could be combined in 46,656 arrangements and then all of the components were derived from these controlling geometries. But it was defined by formal operations and hierarchies not mathematics. Working with moving buildings and building components is a way of designing with algorithms and code for me. This is what is more consistent than the experience of movement.

PRAUD   Form: What are the origins of your firm's name in relation to theory? In its origins was it strictly about studying Topologies which deals more with mathematics, or was there an agenda to study form in relation to its architectural theoretical lineage? For example, one could associate mutations as topological studies, but the Fountain projects or Toy Furniture projects could be associated with Found Form and all the implications that brings.
Not knowing the origins, we would guess that there was already an attitude of pushing architecture in its transition from Cartesian geometry to a topological one. When did you first understand this shift? Was it a software-driven shift or was there already a topological understanding of space even in the analog? (Similar to how you describe Eisenman working computationally in the analog.) The question comes because when we see your earliest work, Stranded Sears Tower from 1992, this is a topological project for

which we are not sure if you were already driven by digital tools, or if it was hand made via a physical model which already required the topological conception of space since the manipulation of bundled tubes can only be understood as a topological problem.

GL   I have always had a reflex to be contrarian and it gets me into trouble. For me, popular culture was, and still is, driven by music. My heroes would turn against anything that was sloppy or debased by popularity, even if it was good. In the late 80s there was a posture taken by journalists against "form." Not by theorists or historians, but by journalists… and then architects who curry favour with journalists. Very similar to the later posture against "starchitects" that caused many architects to describe themselves with clawing false humility. So this is why I chose the term. I am sorry it is as stupid an explanation as that.

MUG = DONUT

"In mathematics, topology is concerned with the properties of a geometric object that are preserved under continuous deformations, such as stretching, twisting, crumpling and bending.
A topological space is a set endowed with a structure, called a Topology, which allows defining continuous deformation of subspaces, and, more generally, all kinds of continuity. Euclidean spaces, and, more generally, metric spaces are examples of a topological space, as any distance or metric defines a Topology. The deformations that are considered in Topology are homeomorphisms and homotopies. A property that is invariant under such deformations is a topological property. Basic examples of topological properties are the dimension, which allows distinguishing between a line and a surface; compactness, which allows distinguishing between a line and a circle; connectedness, which allows distinguishing a circle from two non-intersecting circles."[2]

In mathematics, there is no distinction between a coffee mug and a donut; or a brick and a ball. Scissors would be different from a donut because scissors would have one more perforation in their Topology. As an applicable property in physics, Topology is studied in superfluids, Quantum Hall effect, superconductivity, topological insulators, and string theory. For example, the electrical conductance is greater in objects with more holes in them.

2 "Topology." *Wikipedia*, Wikimedia Foundation, 12 Feb. 2022, https://en.wikipedia.org/wiki/Topology.

77

From donut to cup

MUG = DONUT

ANIMATE FORM

In architecture, the term Topology was appropriated by Greg Lynn with his "Embryological House" project from 1997. At the time, new software in animation had been developed that would allow for volumes to be deformed in order to portray the actions of an animated character. For architecture, it was speculated by Lynn that the computer could generate hundreds of spaces out of the same volume through the animation of its deformations. The Embryological House is a freeze-frame of this process. Each still can be read as a different house, with a different space from the previous iteration, yet it is still the same Topology. Lynn called this the *Animate Form*.[3]

3 Lynn, Greg. *Animate Form*. Princeton Architectural Press, 1998.

Animate Form,
Greg Lynn,
CCA, Canada. 1997–2001

ANIMATE FORM

DE-FORM

Ricardo Bofill's Les quatre barres de la senyera catalana explores topological transformation with a systematic approach. Topologically, the four columns are identical as they maintain the same spatial properties and same typological formation. Each column is composed of four sections, three sections made from a volume primitive box, and one section with a twisted box. However, each column is transformed through the simple placement of the twisted volume section at a specific location of the column. Each column's twist is placed one higher than the previous column. This composition allows for an effect of differentiation, where each column appears to be different from the other.

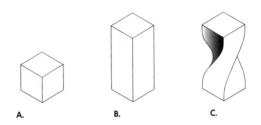

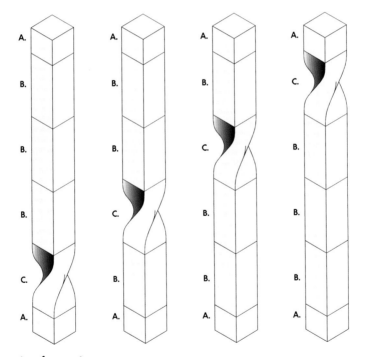

Diagram in reference to:
Les quatre barres de la senyera catalana,
Ricardo Bofill,
Barcelona, Spain. 2009

DE-FORM

SOFT TOPOLOGIES

In art, the works of Kate Scardifield in "Soft Topologies"[4] explore the physical transformations of fabrics as a way to transmit information of movement. "In Soft Topologies many of these pleated fabric sculptures are made from the material used for sails. The sails of a boat; the sails that feel the pull and tug of apparent wind. Within the space of the gallery, these sails are beholden to a different kind of force. Not the force of the North Easterly, but the force of a gesture. Scardifield's pleated textiles have been draped and folded, fanned and collapsed so that their arcs and their contours become something else altogether. And what is it that these sails have become? Studies of form? Well, naturally. But they are also traces."[5]

4 Scardifield, Kate. "Soft Topologies." *KATE SCARDIFIELD*, 2018, https://www.katescardifield.com.au/soft-topologies-text.
5 Philip, Isobel Parker. *The Wind, Apparently*, UTS Gallery, Ultimo, NSW, 2018.

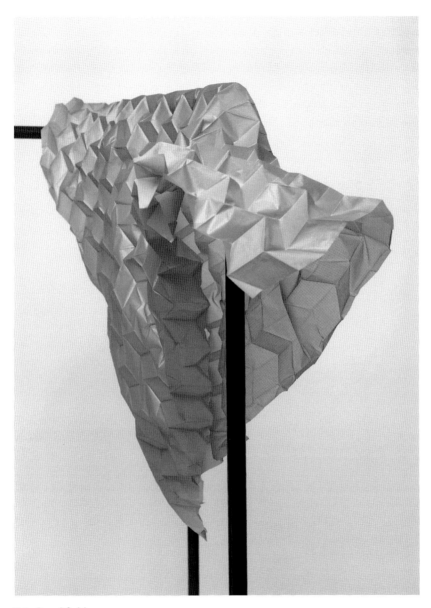

Kate Scardifield,
Soft Topology, 2018,
(Detail) Adaptable sculpture in one variation.
Chevron pleated spinnaker cloth, eyelets, powder coated steel
120 × 148 cm (full expansion)
Photo: Robin Hearfield

SOFT TOPOLOGIES

DIS-ORIENTATION

With no specific orientation assigned to this form, the interior can transform its use simply by tumbling, producing new interior spatial qualities. This exercise on form demonstrates the clear limitations of a planimetric design versus a topological one. Topology is not necessarily bounded by the ground. Mathematically, it is a virtual space defined by points, lines, and surfaces. The user can adapt to the space and assign a function to the space. On the other hand, a planimetric design is bounded by a plane with limited spatial qualities.

85

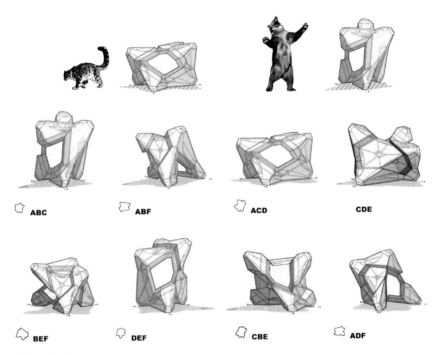

White Elephant,
Bureau Spectacular,
Louisville, USA. 2011

DIS-ORIENTATION

TOPOLOGY AND INTENT

In a choreographed dance, each move of the body has a specific intent. The dancer must interpret the desired intent from the choreographer with their body through contortions and movements of their extremities. Topologically, the human body of the dancer maintains the same topological properties, although its deformations produce different effects. The deformations of volumes in architecture can invoke an intent in form rather than the figurative reading of a shape. The formal intent is meant to achieve an effect within its urban context, just as the dance move is meant to affect the storyline of a ballet in reaction to the musical score.

Body topologies,
PRAUD, 2018

TOPOLOGY AND INTENT

FORMALISM

The 1773 illustrations of Architectural Alphabet by Johann David Steingruber represent a series of formal exercises where Baroque palaces are adapted into the different letters of the alphabet. Although the strategy may seem simple to adapt a "ready-made" form into a pragmatic plan, it questions the relationship between program and form. Although this series of drawings had no practical use, it skillfully demonstrated the malleability of the same function adapted to work in different forms. The relationship between interior spaces is only enhanced through their compression to a formal shell, which maintains a priority for each proposal. Regardless of the fact that the 1773 Architectural Alphabet is represented as a planimetric exercise, the clarity of using a letter as a formal shell allows for a complete break of the Euclidean dynamic as it allows not only the program to adapt to a new form but the same form to adapt to a new context as seen in the "2Y House" by Sebastian Irarrazaval or the "Y House" by Steven Holl. In the latter, the letter form adapts to the topography generating a new space from the same Topology.

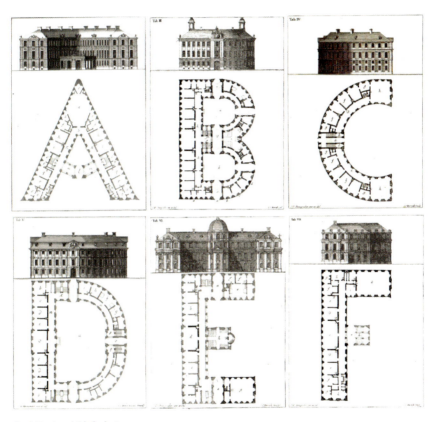

Architectural Alphabet,
Johann David Steingruber, 1773

FORMALISM

PURE FORM

In his book *Von Ledoux bis Le Corbusier. Ursprung und Entwicklung der autonomen Architektur*[6] (From Ledoux to Le Corbusier. Origin and Development of Autonomous Architecture) written in 1933, Emil Kaufmann depicts Claude Nicolas Ledoux, his designs and texts as the beginning of modern architecture. In his analysis of Ledoux' work (and that of his pupils Durand and Debut) he strips away the ornamental classicist "dresses" wrapping his buildings to uncover the revolutionary core of his architecture, the pure form. These forms were depicted as sitting in nature as monumental artifacts that produce their own world. Autonomous to any style, the pure form explores architecture as spatial and not planimetric.

6 Kaufmann, Emil. *Von Ledoux Bis Le Corbusier Ursprung Und Entwicklung Der Autonomen Architektur*. Gerd Hatje, 1985.

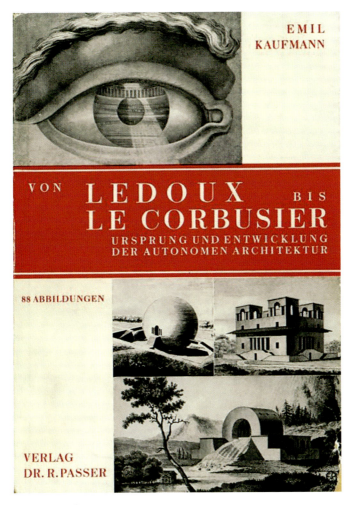

*Von Ledoux bis Le Corbusier.
Ursprung und Entwicklung der autonomen Architektur,*
Emil Kaufman,
Verlag Dr. Rolf Passer, 1933

PURE FORM

CONTEXTUALIZATION

This publication depicts 1,001 forms that were drawn while in three different cities. That is not to say that the forms were representational of the cities, or that they are specific to a particular location. These are urban forms that could be envisioned interchangeably in any urban context. This proposal may be misinterpreted to mean that any form can work in any context in the contemporary architectural scene, hence the name "Siteless,"[7] but the critical point is the possibility to understand the implications that any form can have in creating urban context as a three-dimensional space and not a simple extrusion. Each "siteless" form can potentially be taken as a Found Form that can be contextualized through formal deformations, as the form is submitted to the zoning regulations and code of each site. Hence, form is to be read as a system for generating space.

7 Blanciak François. *Siteless: 1001 Building Forms*. MIT Press, 2008.

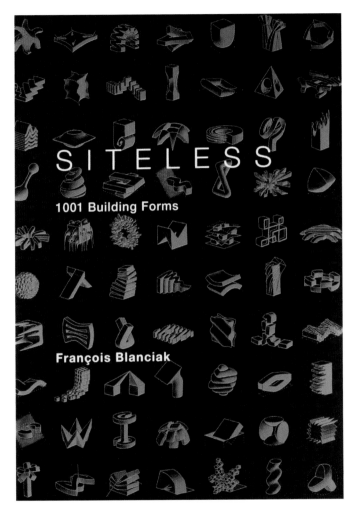

Siteless,
François Blanciak,
MIT Press. 2008

CONTEXTUALIZATION

LEGAL CONTEXTUALIZATION

Legal contextualization has to do with the rules and regulations set by the city where the project is being developed. These follow the zoning codes for floor area ratio (FAR), building coverage ratio (BCR), site boundary, perimeter setbacks, maximum height restriction, maximum number of floors, daylight setbacks, among others, that may pertain to the local jurisdiction. These codes are meant to determine the maximum volume of a building on a particular site without the need for any creative process. The aim is for the city to regulate how building forms can comply with the needs for public health and safety.

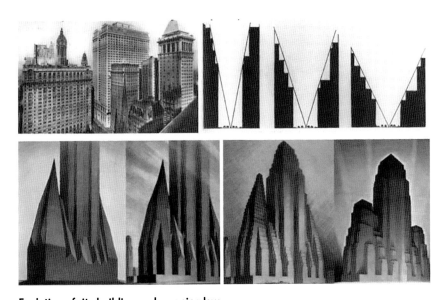

Evolution of city building under zoning law,
Hugh Ferris,
New York City, USA. 1922

URBAN CONTEXTUALIZATION

Urban Contextualization has to do with deformations performed by the architect for the purpose of achieving an urban spatial effect, usually not required by the code parameters. It can be for the purpose of views, daylighting, wind patterns, symbolic axis, among others. This is the case for the West 57 Building by the Bjarke Ingels Group, where a courtyard Topology is hybridized with the podium and tower Topology to achieve views for every unit while also not blocking the neighboring tower. The process for these deformations, although pragmatic in nature, demonstrates the role of the architect in accessing the value for achieving the desired effect beyond the maximum volume prescribed through a legal contextualization.

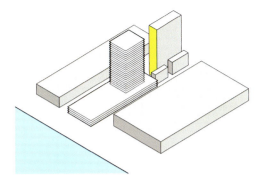

Podium and Tower
- 27 Floors
- 80,000 m²

Implications:
Obstructs the views from the neighbohring tower.

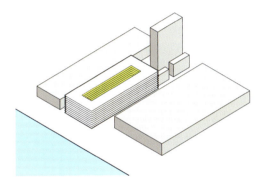

Courtyard
- 10 Floors
- 80,000 m2

Implications:
Some units have an introvert view of the courtyard while others have views to the river.

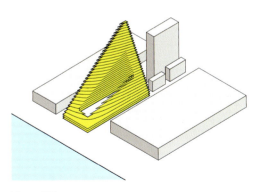

Courtyard Tower
- 35 Floors
- 80,000 m2

Implications:
All units get views, while the neighbohring tower is also not obstructed. The Ground floor can still work as a podium.

Via 57 West,
BIG,
New York City, USA. 2016

URBAN CONTEXTUALIZATION

CONTEXTUAL TRANSFORMATION

The Towada Art Center, the twenty-first-century museum in Kanazawa, and the New Museum in New York are three museums by SANAA where the concept of distributing independent galleries as singular masses is maintained.
The independent gallery concept requires for the autonomy of each gallery to work as a part of the collective where a visitor can experience the idea of a museum by moving from one separate volume to another as opposed to a more traditional sequence of moving between interconnected spaces in a singular volume like the Altes Museum. SANAA proposes the possibility of having a variety of three-dimensional forms form a collective as opposed to a singular shell. The independent gallery concept is tested out on three different contexts, Towada, Kanazawa, and New York, with different site restrictions and parameters. In order for each project to stay true to the concept, the massing must adapt to the context. In Towada, the rectangular urban site surrounded by low-rise buildings forces the galleries to be distributed in a linear configuration in order to fit on the site at ground level. In Kanazawa, sitting in the middle of a park system with a rectangular site of larger proportions, the galleries are grouped through a circular roof providing access from any orientation. In New York, the limited site and verticality of the city forces the stacking of galleries in order to fit the required area within a small footprint. These Contextual Transformations are guided strictly through the clarity of the concept, tying the program to massing, and the massing to a specific site.

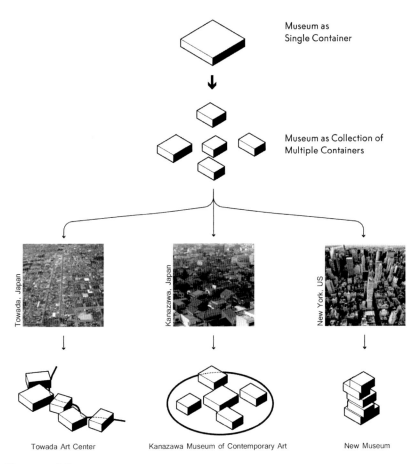

Diagrams of three museums,
SANAA

CONTEXTUAL TRANSFORMATION

OPEN CONTEXT

Overlooking the ocean, the Ochoquebradas House distinguishes itself from the natural context through its monolithic form. Although the forms are autonomous as pure polygons, they are also self-contextual as the formation cuts itself from the openness of the site and demarcates its territory through a horizontal box that serves as a podium. Like a Giacometti sculpture, the podium bounds the sculptural context for the monoliths to act independently as a system of leaning masses.

Casa Ochoquebradas, Alejandro Aravena,
Los Vilos,
Coquimbo Region,
Chile. 2014

OPEN CONTEXT

CLOSED CONTEXT

In an almost monumental quality, Amore Pacific Headquarters adapts to the scale of its urban skyscraper context. Limited by the code parameters of zoning, FAR, BCR, height limitations, and setbacks, this pure form assumes a phenomenological transformation of carving out courtyards in order to create views as a connection to the greater context and sky courtyards. This relationship between Amore Pacific HQ and the context purely comes from the formal parameters set by the context rather than its program. This implies an assumption that the same form could have been achieved regardless of the proposed program.

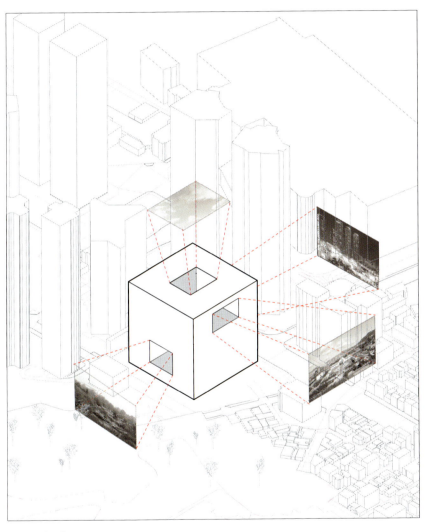

Amore Pacific,
David Chipperfield,
Seoul, Korea. 2017

CLOSED CONTEXT

CONNOTATION/DENOTATION

In Bruno Munari's toy set of building wooden blocks for kids, *Scatola di Architettura*,[8] a set of seven block types form the palette for building a church, a palace, a factory, a school, a house, among other building types. A kid, without having endured the rigorous academic training of a seasoned architect, knows these forms to be building types from the various compositions of the block elements, implying that form has a connotation of building type. If not, the denotation of the form would just read as a pile of wooden blocks no matter the configuration.

8 Munari, Bruno. *Scatola Di Architettura MC 1*. Corraini, 2003.

Scatola di Architettura,
Bruno Munari,
Corraini Edizioni, 1945

CONNOTATION/DENOTATION

SIGN LANGUAGE

Imagine the character of "Thing" from the Addams Family to be real. The character is a severed hand that still moves and relies on the motion of its fingers to communicate. Its topological properties are always the same, and its "signifier" is a human hand. Yet, depending on the way that it transforms to communicate and move, the "signified" reading is different. Just like sign language, the hand can gesture letters of the alphabet, compliments, rude gestures, salutations, and insults. All of these signs are achieved from the same Topology being submitted to different transformations as seen in the *Supplemento al Dizionario Italiano*[9] by Bruno Munari.

9 Munari, Bruno. *Supplemento Al Dizionario Italiano*. Muggiani, 1963.

107

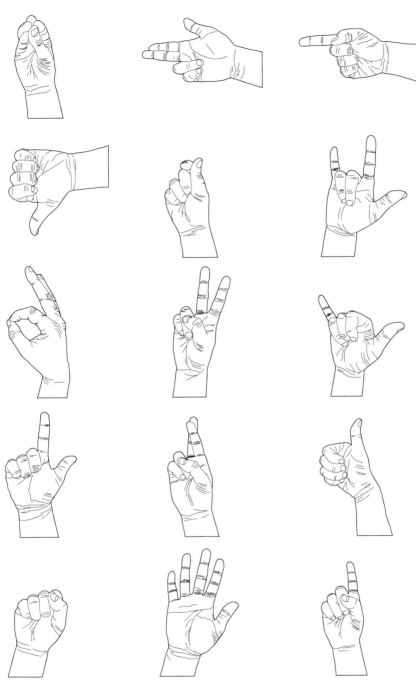

Diagram of sign language in reference to:
Supplemento al dizionario Italiano,
Bruno Munari,
Corraini Edizioni, 1963

SIGN LANGUAGE

SEMIOTICS

Postmodernism struggled with the sterility of modernism, which led to borrowing historic architectural symbols being applied to modern construction systems. This need to create a perception of a historical artifact with meaning also relied on facadism, questioning the integrity of the symbolism of such an image. In their 1972 publication, *Learning from Las Vegas*,[10] Venturi, Brown, Izenour proposed the bold statement that architecture is dependent on its perception, past experiences, and emotional associations, which may not coincide with a building's form, system, or program; "Image over form or process."

This proposal is manifested in two conditions: a building that acts as a symbolic form (the Duck) or a building that acts as a scaffolding for symbols to be applied to it through ornamentation (the Decorated Shed).

The Duck, represented by a building in a shape of a duck, deforms its system and program toward achieving a symbolic form. For example, a building in the shape of a basket to house the offices of a basket-making company.

The Decorated Shed, on the other hand, would fit the program into any system as an ornamental symbol is applied independently of the form to announce its function. In dense cities like Tokyo or Seoul, generic buildings are covered completely with billboards in order to advertise the programs happening inside, masquerading the actual building. The shed defies the importance of form as "Architecture is a shelter with symbols on it."

10 Venturi, Robert, et al. *Learning from Las Vegas*. The MIT Press, 2017, pp. 87–91.

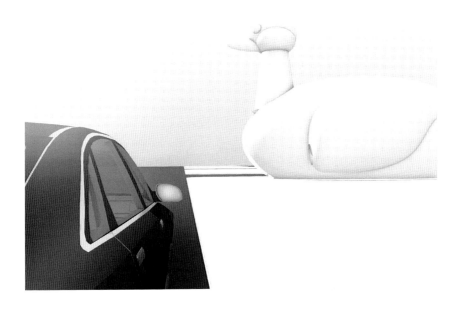

Renderings of car approaching two restairants. In reference to:
Learning from Las Vegas,
Robert Venturi,
Denise Scott Brown & Steven Izenour,
MIT Press, 1972

SEMIOTICS

SIGNIFIED AND SIGNIFIER

At the Jewish Museum in Berlin, Daniel Libeskind purposefully uses the Topology of an extruded Star of David to deform it into a zigzag bar that signifies the historical paths of Jewish life in Germany. The Topology is trying to communicate the museum's narrative in order for the building itself to be an experiential exhibit rather than an exhibition of artifacts. It must be understood then that the selection of massing has implications in the context not as a practical matter but as part of a semiotic system of signifiers. The contortion of the Topology must comply with the local building codes for legal contextualization but the driver for deformation is a phenomenological contextualization.

111

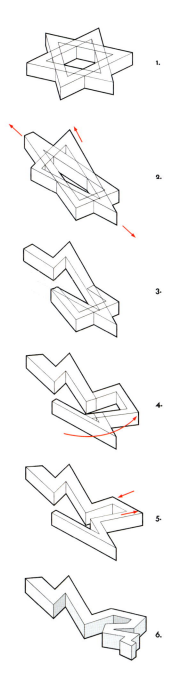

Jewish Museum Berlin,
Daniel Libeskind, Berlin,
Germany. 2001

SIGNIFIED AND SIGNIFIER

ADOPTED FORM

There are distinct Collective Forms that are associated with being successful urban spaces due to their formal qualitative properties. Such is the case for Piazza San Marco in Venice, Bedford Square in London, Il Campo in Siena, Piazza San Pietro in the Vatican, among other spaces from around the world. If these open public spaces are abstracted to their pure form, deprived of ornamentation or style, then they can be understood as urban topologies. They can be studied through their proportions, scale, formal relationships between solid and void. These formal properties could then be transplanted into another context to produce urban spaces with the same spatial quality. Such is the claim that Colin Rowe and Fred Koetter make in their book *Collage City*.[11] Established urban forms can be adopted for a different context without copying the architecture but its figure-ground.

11 Rowe, Colin, and Fred Koetter. *Collage City*. Birkhäuser, 2009.

A. Piazza San Marco, Venice
B. Champ de Mars, Paris
C. Bedford Square, London
D. Piazza San Pietro, Vatican
E. Piazza del Campo, Siena
F. Jardin du Palais Royal, Paris

Collage City – Gangnam,
PRAUD,
Seoul, Korea. 2020

ADOPTED FORM

COURTYARDS

In architecture, the topological gestures and transformations are still bound by pragmatic orders. They cannot be as radical as in a clay form that could transform a donut into a mug. However, the radicality in architecture may come from the re-appropriation of a banal form and its re-orientation under a new perspective. For instance, MVRDV's Mirador Housing in Madrid is based on a typical courtyard housing block Topology of Madrid where different buildings infill the entire perimeter of the block to form such a courtyard. Conceptually, the courtyard configuration formed by perimeter buildings is tilted vertically so as to now have the form of the courtyard in the sky. The public space, which originally consisted of only sidewalks, is now transformed into open ground. The courtyard remains as a private collective space for the residences, maintaining its original topological purpose.

1.
Courtyard Massing
Following the typical massing model of the neighborhood

2.
Tilting Courtyard
The whole block is tilted up in order to provide more public space.

3.
Massing Adjustments
The block is moved back and proportioned to create an axial relationship to the main road.

4.
Sky Courtyard
The final result provided connections to the mountains, terminus for the main road axis, and more public grounds.

Mirador,
MVRDV,
Madrid, Spain. 2005

COURTYARDS

ABSOLUTE FORM

In his book, *The Possibility of an Absolute Architecture*,[12] Pier Vitorio Aureli describes an architecture that distances itself from the rest of the context. This distanciation is produced by a clear formal boundary, a demarcation, a cut from the urban context. The aim is to establish some sense of architectural order within the urban sea by forming an architectural island. Aureli discusses the use of the podium in the works of Mies van der Rohe as one of the strategies, or the monumental pure form in the works of Etienne Louis Boullée. Analogous to a fortress wall in a medieval city, DOGMA exercises that absoluteness through an 800-m by 800-m wall housing form that produces its own urban logic within its own perimeter in "A Simple Heart." All these projects demarcate a clear boundary between inside and outside the form, which produces its own urbanity inside. "Walled Gardens" enclose green ecologies that are protected by an architectural wall within the dense city of Seoul.

12 Aureli, Pier Vittorio. *The Possibility of an Absolute Architecture*. MIT Press, 2011.

Walled Gardens,
PRAUD,
Seoul, 2022

ABSOLUTE FORM

COLLECTIVE FORM: (COMPOSITIONAL FORM)

In Fumihiko Maki's essay on Collective Form,[13] a paradigm shift is suggested from theories of the individual form to an analysis of Collective Forms that shape our cities with an element of time. He brings forward the idea that cities need to cope with the changing modern scales of mega highways and the disparate form caused by their growth. Architects have adopted a sense of trying to achieve a unique building that outdoes the previous one, generating an eclectic cityscape with not much of an urban composition. For that reason, there should be an analytical study of the Collective Form that could restore a formal order to the city. Maki distinguishes three approaches to the Collective Form theory made up of the compositional form, the megaform, and the group form.

The compositional form is predetermined by the designer as a collection of building components. "It is a static approach, because the act of making a composition itself has a tendency to complete a formal statement."[14] Ville Radieuse proposed the radical transformation of Paris through the redevelopment of the city as a highly organized repetitive composition of high-rise buildings in a tabula rasa setting. Based on his Utopian vision of Ville Contemporaine for three million people, Le Corbusier sought the perfect form through geometrical repetition and symmetry. In an almost totalitarian order, the different typologies of buildings are pre-arranged based on the architect's logic forming an overall composition of the city. The architect has control over every formal aspect of the urban space, leaving no room for serendipitous urbanization.

13 Maki, Fumihiko. *Investigations in Collective Form*. School of Architecture, Washington University, 2004.
14 Ibid., p. 6.

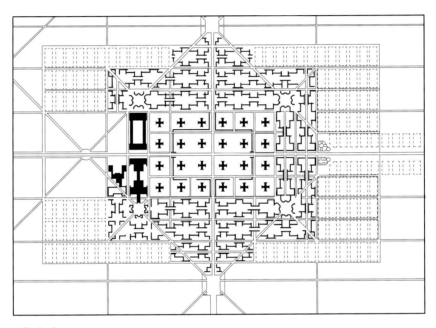

Ville Radieuse,
Le Corbusier,
Paris, France. 1924

COLLECTIVE FORM: (COMPOSITIONAL FORM)

COLLECTIVE FORM: (MEGAFORM)

Maki's second strategy for the Collective Form mentions the megaform, described as a large framework that houses all the components of the city.[15] It is inherently static, and it tends to concentrate functions. Maki's criticism deals with the megaform's inability to deal with the rapid change of technology through time, and might become obsolete. Instead, the megaform should work like a megastructure that can expand or contract offering flexibility of change. Its best potential attributes are environmental engineering, multi-functional structures, and infrastructure as public investment.

The megaform allowed for the architect to engage the scale of the city through singular gestures as seen in Japp Bakemas' proposal for Tel Aviv.[16] An architectural spine runs through the entire center of the city in order to organize it with a singular readable form.

15 Maki, Fumihiko. *Investigations in Collective Form*. School of Architecture, Washington University, 2004, p. 8.
16 "Het Nieuwe Instituut." *Objects*, https://zoeken.hetnieuweinstituut.nl/en/objects/deta il/?q=Bakema+Tel+Aviv&page=2.

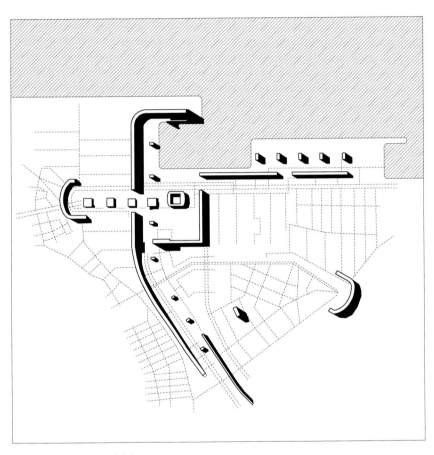

Nieuw Stadscentrum Tel Aviv,
Bakema van den Broek,
Tel Aviv, Israel. 1963

COLLECTIVE FORM: (MEGAFORM)

COLLECTIVE FORM: (GROUP FORM)

The group form is described as the newest conceptual strategy for Maki's Collective Form. "It is form which evolves from a system of generative elements in space."[17] Unlike the megaform, which Maki describes as needing a skeleton to frame growth, the group form is a system of elements that follow an underlying code, resulting in an overall form that evolves over time. Maki shows the Japanese linear village, a medieval city, and a Greek mountain village as examples of group forms. The individual element has an inherent rule that allows its attachment to the system.

In Maki's own Hillside Terrace, the architect is allowed to engage the growth of the neighborhood through multiple interventions throughout many decades. The different phases of the project allow for Maki's interventions to evolve as new buildings are placed, reflecting the construction technology of the time. This pseudo organic growth maintains the overall organizational structure of the neighborhood over many decades.

17 Maki, Fumihiko. *Investigations in Collective Form*. School of Architecture, Washington University, 2004, p. 14.

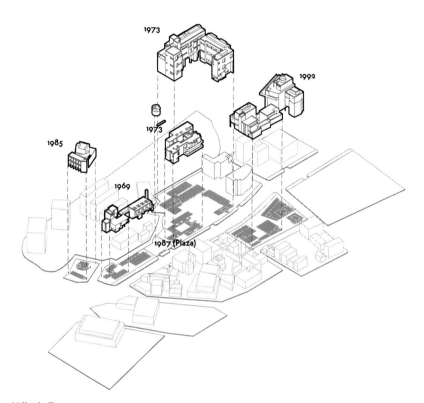

Hillside Terrace,
Fumihiko Maki,
Tokyo, Japan. 1969–1992

COLLECTIVE FORM: (GROUP FORM)

CITY AS TOPOLOGIES

A study on the housing market of Phoenix, AZ, revealed a variety of housing unit types despite the contrary idea of housing being monotonous in the area. As a topological study, the traditional housing type with a front- and backyard is inverted into a courtyard Topology. In order to produce variability in the urban fabric, these topological courtyard formations are parametrized to a parcelization process based on land radiation heat maps rather than a zoning plan. This produces a plan that reflects solar land value where the topologies can expand or contract based on the occupancy levels that each parcel can provide.[18]

18 Trummer, Peter. "Peter Trummer (February 22, 2012)." *YouTube*, SCI-Arc Media Archive, 7 Sept. 2017, https://youtu.be/UCbf9P9dySY.

AD Phoenix/Arizona
Credits: Peter Trummer
Associative Design Project: Urban Ecology_Phoenix Arizona 2007/2008
@Berlage Institute Rotterdam.
Model: Lin Chia-ring, Mika Watanabe.
Photo: Peter Tijhuis
Image Courtesy: Peter Trummer

CITY AS TOPOLOGIES

HYBRID FORM

"The Cadavre Exquis (Exquisite Corpse) was a favourite
surrealist game from the mid-1920s onwards. It usually
involved three or four participants who added to a
drawing, collage or sentence, without seeing what the
others had already done. This work is one of several
made by Breton, his second wife Jacqueline Lamba,
and Yves Tanguy, while on a weekend holiday together
in February 1938. However, this piece might have been
made collaboratively rather than by folding the paper
to hide the previous contribution, since there are no fold
lines on the paper"[19]

(National Galleries of Scotland).

The fusion of different typological parts allows for the composition of
a new whole form. The merger of different typologies produces the
effect of authenticity in form, which cannot be described through a
single stylistic reading. The focus on form and not style differentiates
this technique from an eclectic stylistic composition. The selection of
unique formal parts is a spatial approach where form does not need to
follow any specific function, but rather a spatial effect. Its composition
may very well be random. The same can be said in architecture through
the production of a Frankenstein building made up of a fusion of forms.
The Taipei Performing Arts Center by OMA, for example, produces this
effect through the aggregation of different theater typological forms
grouped as one building.

19 Breton, Andre, et al. "Cadavre Exquis [Exquisite Corpse]." *National Galleries of
Scotland*, National Galleries of Scotland, 2020, https://www.nationalgalleries.org/art-
and-artists/31332/cadavre-exquis-exquisite-corpse.

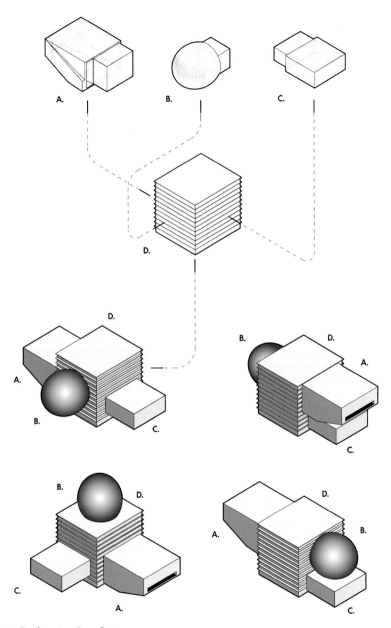

Taipei Performing Arts Center,
OMA,
Taipei, Taiwan 2022

HYBRID FORM

FOUND FORM

Analogous to Pop-Art and the "ready-made" works, the New York Museum of Modern Art exhibited "Architectural Fantasies"[20] in 1967, showcasing the works of Walter Pichler, Hans Hollein, and Raimund Abraham. Hollein's contribution depicted montages of enlarged familiar objects inserted into landscapes. This can be interpreted as a direct critique of modernism and indirectly to Louis Sullivan's "form follows function." This series of collage projects brought a critical perspective of form in architecture just as ready-made became critical in art. By enlarging everyday objects to the scale of buildings, Hollein was immediately producing the sense of a new spatial logic that could not be conceived by the modernist system. Form becomes architectural through scale, not through function. The scaling of a screw or an electrical plug to the scale of a building and placed in the landscape engendered an autonomy in architecture where the form could be re-appropriated regardless of function.

The composition of an object defines certain edges in space, which can be described as the formal properties of an object. These properties can be studied deprived of any style or function; form for form's sake. This is a critical point for understanding form in architecture as a departure from modernist tendencies in association to function.

20 *Museum of Modern Art.* MoMA, https://assets.moma.org/documents/moma_press-release_326503.pdf.

A. Cheese Grater
B. Plug Adapter
C. Toblerone
D. Donut
E. Tumbler
F. Modem
G. Headphones
H. Beach Ball
I. Space Heater

 A.
 B.
 C.
 D.
 E.
 F.
 G.
 H.
 I.

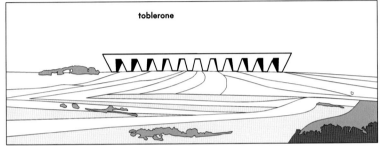
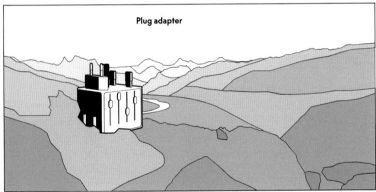
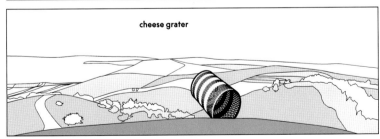

Diagrams of objects in landscape in reference to:
Highrise Building, Sparkplug Project,
Hans Hollein,
MoMA, USA. 1964.

FOUND FORM

FORM OVER FUNCTION

In 1971, the Museum of Modern Art in New York exhibited "Education of an Architect: A Point of View."[21] This was an exhibition curated by John Hejduk showcasing the works of 50 students from Cooper Union. The aim was to demonstrate a new pedagogical attitude toward the advancement of architecture that would question "1) The Problem of Mass; 2) The Problem of Method; 3) The Problem of Physical Design; and 4) The Problem of the Architect: His Future Education." The exhibition intended to disrupt the modernist techniques of functionalism and guide students toward the plasticity of form. Among many of Hejduk's exercises that rejected any preconceptions of form, Hejduk's students were asked to solve problems such as the nine squares and the cube. They would also go through the process of interpreting an abstract painting into a house, for example. The end result would yield forms and spaces that would have to get appropriated with a specific program regardless of the form.

21 *Museum of Modern Art.* MoMA, https://assets.moma.org/documents/moma_press-release_326374.pdf.

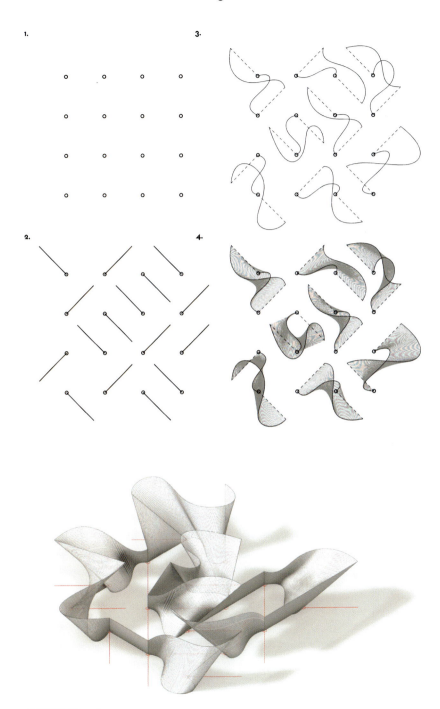

9 SQUARE Exercise,
Student exercise,
Seoul. 2021

FORM OVER FUNCTION

"WE'LL HAVE ONE OF EACH"

Stirling's typological study is not the solution to the WZB puzzle. While the final project is undoubtedly an extension of its discoveries, the choice of the five specific buildings is revealed to be inconsequential. They could have been the building types depicted in the sketch but not ultimately 'chosen,' or they could have been any other building type within architectural history. A basilica is no more appropriate for a social science office building than a medieval keep or a palazzo. All of history is made available to the architect, but that history is rendered ahistorical.[22] The random selection of typological forms to be used for the WZB offices demonstrates the flexibility that a program can have adapting to any form. Office spaces could be envisioned working in a cathedral space, the keep, or palazzo since function is formless. Changing the physical setting where the same function is performed produces a new perception of the space as a new typology. In 1981, Bernard Tschumi had theorized on the dissociation of program from its shell through the process of crossprogramming, disprogramming, and transprogramming in his book *The Manhattan Transcripts*.[23]

22 Reeser, Amanda. "'We'll Have One of Each.'" *Canadian Centre for Architecture*, CCA, https://www.cca.qc.ca/en/articles/issues/25/a-history-of-references/56241/well-have-one-of-each.
23 Tschumi, Bernard. *The Manhattan Transcripts*. Academy Editions, 1981.

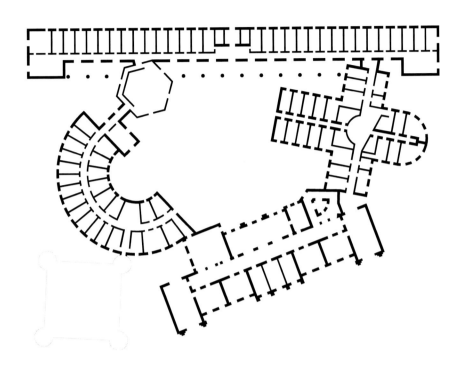

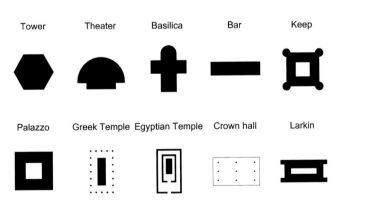

WZB, James Stirling,
Berlin,
Germany. 1988

"WE'LL HAVE ONE OF EACH"

PROGRAMMATIC ELEMENT

Function does not have to follow form, but program can be associated or assigned to a form for the purpose of producing physical relationships between the different required spaces of a project. By assigning a form to a specific program, program in itself becomes an architectural spatial element. The proposal for the Très Grande Bibliothèque (1989) and the realized Seattle Public Library (1999–2004) evidence this notion. In both projects, the program is assigned to a platonic form. Treated as objects, the programmatic elements are then held up and separated from each other, forming in-between spaces (third spaces not required by the project's program brief).

For the Seattle Central Library, this strategy presented the possibility of re-conceptualizing the role of a library as a civic space, part of the social realm.[24] The separation of the required program allowed to produce in-between social spaces that achieve transforming the library not only as a classic collection of knowledge through books, but as a contemporary collector of information through social interaction and various media.

24 Werlemann, Hans, et al. *Seattle Public Library*. OMA/LMN, 2001.

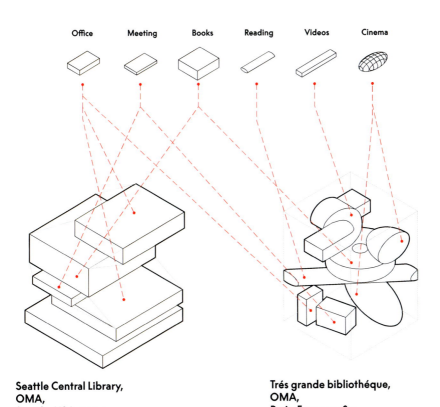

Seattle Central Library,
OMA,
Seattle, USA, 2004

Diagrams of program as form.

Trés grande bibliothéque,
OMA,
Paris, France, 1989

PROGRAMMATIC ELEMENT

FORM AS SYSTEM

As described by OMA, the Y2K house had a particular client that demanded a house where the users could have separate spaces while living together.[25] The massing strategy became one of carving out a mass in order to create the shared space. Although the project only reached the conceptual stage, the massing strategy became a methodology for space making, regardless of program, a system that could be adapted under other parameters. One year later in 1999, the Casa da Musica was commissioned in Porto. Both projects, different in scale and program, explore the premise of a void occupying the dominant space carved out of a mass. In the house, the living room becomes the void that unites all, and in the Casa da Musica, the main concert hall takes over the void space, using the city as a performance backdrop. Form proved to be systematic as the void and solid spaces were adjusted based on the scale of the required program and site conditions.

25 "Y2K House." OMA, https://www.oma.com/projects/y2k-house.

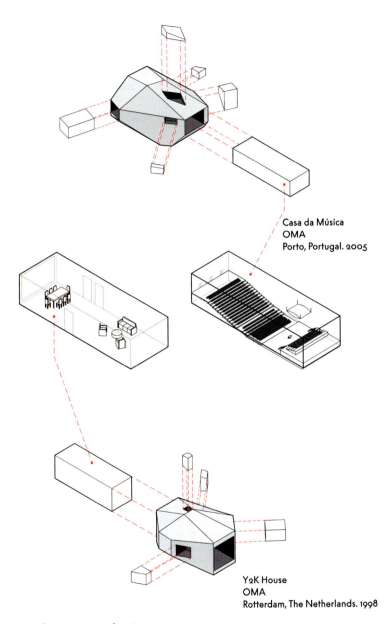

Casa da Música
OMA
Porto, Portugal. 2005

Y2K House
OMA
Rotterdam, The Netherlands. 1998

Diagram of two projects showing
the same formal system.

FORM AS SYSTEM

PARTS TO WHOLE

Arranged as two separate puzzles, two distinct houses are composed from a set of five autonomous forms. Each house shares the same "kit of parts" arranged in a different configuration to produce a Hexagon house and a Square house. The formal autonomy of each piece as unique topologies produces non-planar adjacencies on what otherwise would be single-story homes once all the parts configure a whole.

139

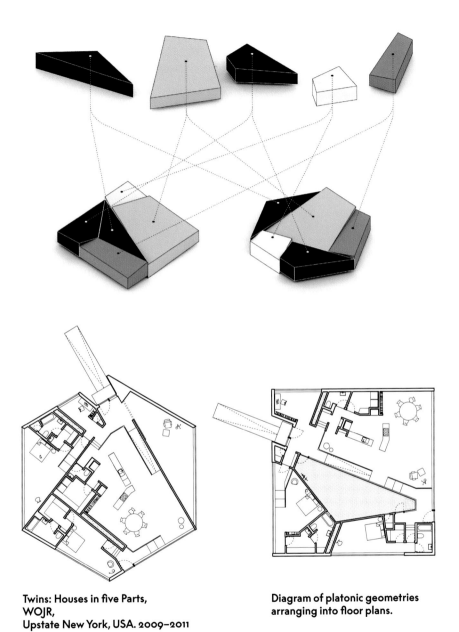

Twins: Houses in five Parts,
WOJR,
Upstate New York, USA. 2009–2011

Diagram of platonic geometries
arranging into floor plans.

PARTS TO WHOLE

FIGURE-GROUND

While explaining the predicament of texture, Rowe and Koetter present a few examples for figures and their emplacement in the urban context that serve as texture (urban fabric), yet maintain internal freedom.[26] These are the Palazzo Farnese, Palazzo Borghese, and the Hotel de Beauvais. These buildings have a similar response to adjusting their perimeters to the site conditions while maintaining an inner courtyard that complies with the building type. This presents a duality of the building acting as an urban fabric generator as well as a formal object that offers an additional interior construct. As a two-dimensional representation, these buildings control their domain in relation to the ground. Hence, the methodology of figure-ground is used to represent formal aspects of this type to understand a building and its relationship to the urban context.

26 Rowe, Colin, and Fred Koetter. *Collage City*. Birkhäuser, 2009.

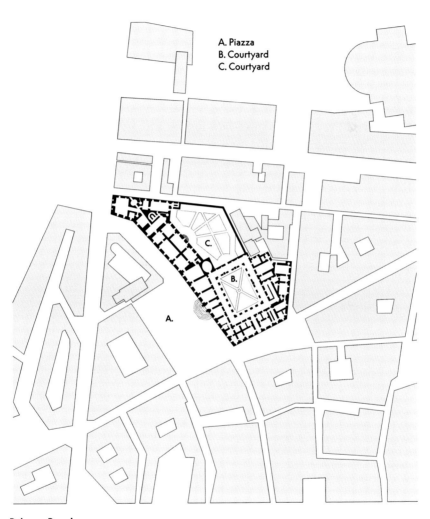

A. Piazza
B. Courtyard
C. Courtyard

Palazzo Borghese,
Rome, Italy. 1560

FIGURE-GROUND

GROUNDFIGURE

The methodology of figure-ground discussed in "Collage City" proposed an architecture that could engage the city through its formal reading as a private figure that can also arrange public ground. This planimetric proposition assumed that buildings are confined to this singular reading. Projects like "Talponia" by Gabetti e Isola from 1968 integrate temporary workers' housing into a hill, hiding the massing as public space above. The conceptual proposition by SITE from 1976 hides a supermarket under a parking carpet, undulating the ground in order to fill the ground with the supermarket program. These projects show the condition where the relationship of the figure-ground is lost as the ground is used to produce the figure. Advances in technology at the turn of the century allowed for further explorations of this concept. Mecanoo's TU Delft Library in 1998 and more ambitiously Peter Eisenman's Santiago de Compostela manipulate the ground as the programmatic figure.

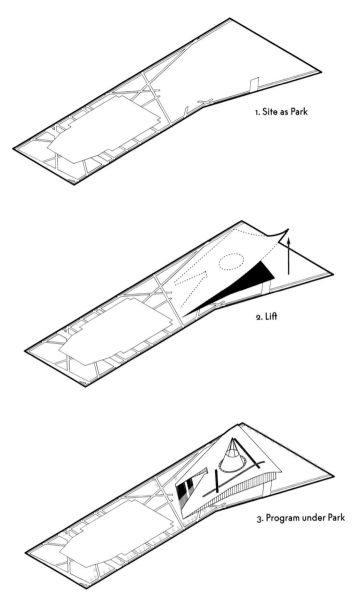

1. Site as Park
2. Lift
3. Program under Park

TU Delft Library,
Mecanoo, Delft,
The Netherlands. 1998

GROUNDFIGURE

UNANCHORED

During the 1950s and 1960s, Yona Friedman envisioned an urban space frame that could occupy the air rights over underutilized spaces of cities.[27] He presented a photomontage drawing of this space frame spanning over rail yards in Paris, infilled with white boxes that would plug in between the space frame as habitable spaces. The premise of occupying the skies has a larger implication for architecture becoming more topological rather than a vertical stacking of horizontal planes confined to a parcel. By unanchoring architecture to explore topologies that address the sky as much as the ground, a new public realm can be created. A more topological approach was explored by El Lissitzky's constructivists project Wolkenbügel from 1924, where a single building would occupy different corners of an intersection by spanning over the road. Metabolists like Arata Isozaki and his "City in the Air" from 1962 also envisioned structures that would aggregate in the sky supported by a single core. Aside from the structural challenges that these projects faced during their time, they proposed a radical idea of air rights as a space that can be constructed in multiple directions. By understanding the city as a three-dimensional volume rather than a planimetric surface, the urban experience becomes more spatial.

27 Friedman, Yona. *Yona Friedman: Pro Domo.* ACTAR, 2006.

145

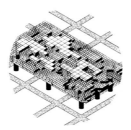

Cloud Project
El Lissitzky (1924)

Spatial City
Yona Friedman (1958)

Cluster in the Air,
Arata Isozaki (1962)

Intrapolis
Walter Jonas (1964)

Architecture Principe,
Derivation Site
Claude Parent (1966)

Sharp Center for Design of
OCAD
Will Alsop (2004)

Axonometrics of six examples of unanchored projects using
air rights to produce three-dimensional blocks.

UNANCHORED

GROUND

Architecture has an intrinsic relationship to the ground, the ground being a highly charged field that can demarcate boundaries based on how architecture interacts with it. Architecture can politicize the ground by making it free for all to use, or it can make it inaccessible. Architecture can extend the public ground into the building, and vice versa, or divert it. Architecture can separate itself from the ground, levitating over it, or be completely formed by it. Ground is topological, not planar; hence, its relationship to architecture is achieved through its deformation and spatial properties. This relationship is also a reflection of the context, be it social, economical, political, or cultural. Le Corbusier's Villa Savoye (1931) separated itself from the ground as the "machine for living" dominated over the landscape in the era of rapid industrialization. City of Culture of Galicia (2011) by Peter Eisenman, on the other hand, forms the building from topographical manipulations of ground vectors. Zaha Hadid's Rosenthal Center for Contemporary Art (2003) extends the city's ground into the building as the ground tilts vertically, while Will Alsop's Sharp Centre (2004) separates itself by floating above the ground.

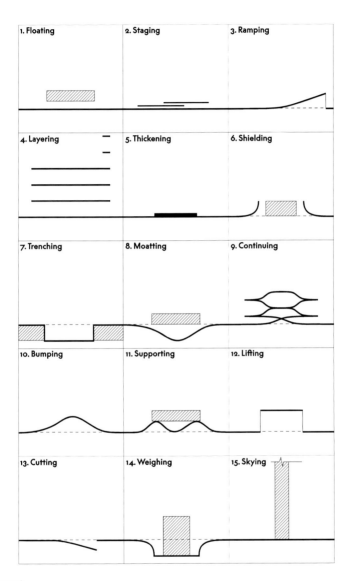

GROUNDS

GROUND

GROUNDSCAPE

Designed in 1995 and completed in 2002, the Yokohama Ferry Terminal can be summarized as an extension of the city looping onto an existing pier. The public ground is manipulated through sections that control security checkpoints versus public access while avoiding the notion of rooms. Rather than rooms, the building is composed of grounds that interlace as a continuous vector. This 430-m-long infrastructural facility masks its highly technical requirements by hybridizing public urban space with the infrastructure of the international passenger terminal.

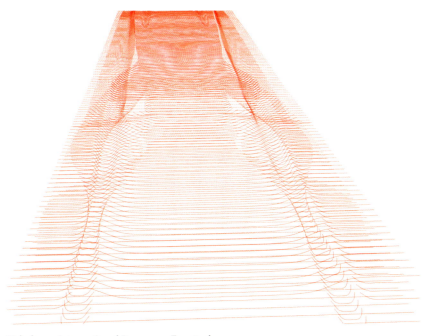

Yokohama International Passenger Terminal,
FOA,
Yokohama, Japan. 2002

THE OBLIQUE

In a radical criticism of the modernist discontinuity in space, Claude Parent along with Paul Virilio introduced "the function of the oblique." Seeking to destabilize the mechanical order of modernism, the oblique presents an active alternative for exploring continuities through the inclined plane. A variety of models and drawings investigated functional displacement through the incline, producing tilting buildings and hexagonal cell planes that blended urban dwellings and circulation as an urban continuity.

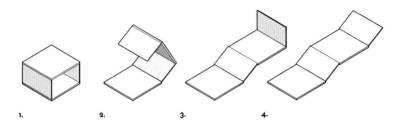

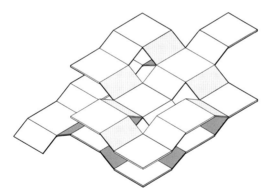

Diagram of a modernist box unfolding to use all
surfaces as a connected ground. In reference to:
la fonction oblique, Claude Parent,
France. 1965–1967

THE OBLIQUE

FIGURE-SKY

Envisioned as an infinite Möbius strip, the vertical volume is submitted to several twisting transformations resulting in a prismatic torus-like high-rise. Although the project was not built and only reached a conceptual stage, it presented an ambition to treat a skyscraper as a three-dimensional form and not just an extrusion of a figure. Rather than a simple silhouette against the background of the sky, the figure-sky relationship becomes volumetric.

Highrise as an
Extrusion of the
parcel

Highrise as a Topology
on the skyline

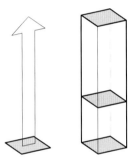
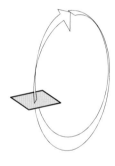
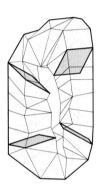

Max Reinhardt Haus,
Peter Eisenman,
Berlin,
Germany. 1992

FIGURE-SKY

URBAN FRAME

As a significant project that welcomed the new millennium, Rem Koolhaas took an interest in developing a new formal urban expression that moved beyond the worn-out "exclamation mark" gesture that had plagued skyscrapers for a century.

Mostly extrusions of their footprint, reflections of capitalism rather than of their urban context, skyscrapers have mainly followed a typical formula as a form that competes for its place in the skyline through height. Meanwhile, the CCTV uses its "bigness" as a contorted donut form to provide an urban frame to the city and its citizens at an urban scale. This unstable form, unlike most other skyscrapers that show off their rigid verticality, suggests a new way of understanding the relationship between a skyscraper and an imperfect urban context as the frames change depending on the angle at which the CCTV is seen from.

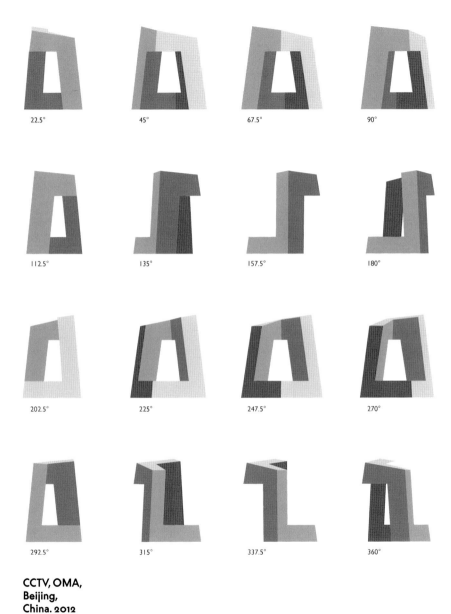

CCTV, OMA,
Beijing,
China. 2012

URBAN FRAME

FIGURE NO GROUND

Perhaps Will Alsop's OCAD is one of the critical projects that achieved the concept of "flying architecture" postulated by revolutionary architects such as Yona Friedman, El Lissizky, or Walter Jonas that conceptualized the use of air rights with horizontal buildings. They were often conceived as paper architects as the construction technology was not advanced enough to realize their projects. This factor has radically changed in the twenty-first century with advancements in modeling software, structural analysis, and material technology as seen in projects like Steven Holl's Vanke Center (2009) and the Sifang Art Museum (2011).

Will Alsop was a firm believer in preserving the different layers of the city by avoiding demolitions of any of its buildings.[28] Though the OCAD presented difficulties in accessibility and structure, this flying mass takes a unique approach to contextualization by floating above the existing fabric, forming a gateway entrance to the public park. A ground-level massing would have probably not achieved the integration between the private facilities and public connections that the OCAD did.

28 "Will Alsop – Nothing Is Lost." *YouTube*, 9 Oct. 2015, https://youtu.be/OSFgWR7Qepg.

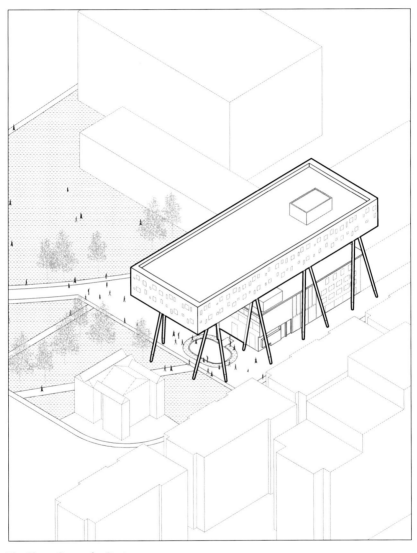

The Sharp Center for Design,
Will Alsop,
Toronto, Canada. 2004

FIGURE NO GROUND

TOPOLOGIES OF CONTAINMENT

The deformation of Topology in architecture is meant to produce a dialogue with its context by means of its relationship to the ground. Arguably, one way that architecture can be political is through its manipulation of the ground and the way a topological formation can raise it, cut it, enclose it, continue it, or extend it, producing definitions of privacy, publicness, or a blurring of both through a third space. The third space is unaccounted for in the program; it is an architectural maneuver of the massing to produce extra collective space.

TOPOLOGIES OF CONTAINMENT

1. Elevated
2. Courtyard
3. Quad
4. In-between
5. Piling
6. Implied Enclosure (Corners/ Points)
7. Implied Enclosure (Boundaries/ Lines)
8. Bowl
9. Interior Courtyard
10. U
11. Tunnel
12. O
13. Sky Boundary
14. Horizon
15. Layering
16. Catcher's Mitt

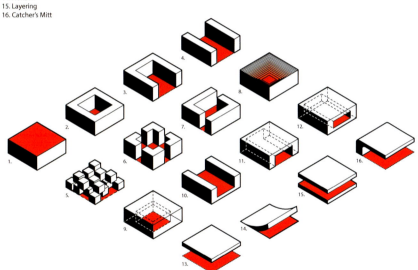

The Third Space,
PRAUD

TOPOLOGIES OF CONTAINMENT

TUNNEL THIRD SPACE

Market Hall in Rotterdam forms a tunnel apartment block that shelters a public square that functions as a public market for most of the day, and it transforms into a lit public square after hours. By allowing a synergy between the private sector development of apartments and the public sector to inject a market within it, it creates a catalyst for urban renewal in the area. Public markets are usually designated around the city as part of a food management infrastructure, taking over prime real estate. In this model, real estate can be maximized through a spatial duality.

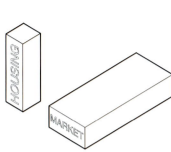
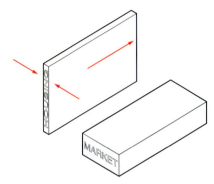

1. Program Massing

2. Program Massing Manipulation

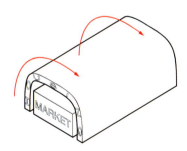
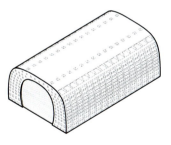

3. Deformation

4. Market Housing

Markethal,
MVRDV,
Rotterdam, The Netherlands. 2014

TUNNEL THIRD SPACE

LAWN THIRD SPACE

This project presents the potential for reevaluating the importance of social infrastructure within the framework of the city. The Edu-carpet is a proposal in Seoul where an education center building integrates its massing to the open space as a larger urban plaza that rolls up into a vertical building. On the street side, this building will face the future US Embassy, meaning that the street side will be a barrier. The building acknowledges this imminent future situation and opens to the north, where it can be integrated into the neighborhood as part of an open system of public spaces. The vertical building will house all the private office spaces while underneath the plaza will hold all the public amenities and programs like an auditorium and classes. This project has a strong agenda for the public realm outside the building as much as inside.

1. Existing site

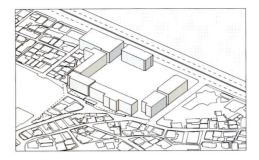

2. Opening of the site

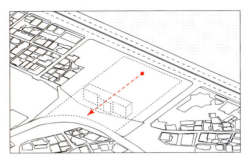

3. Lifting of the ground to match the surrounding development height.

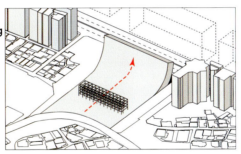

4. Ground as building and public space as one.

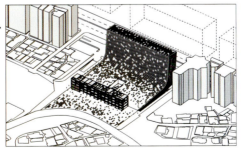

SEOUL Edu-Carpet,
PRAUD,
Seoul, Korea, 2018.

LAWN THIRD SPACE

TYPO

Index Part 2

OGY

The fundamental 'type' of the circular shrine for instance, is independent of the function, sometimes complex, which such buildings must fulfill. It was only in the second half of the nineteenth century that an attempt was made to set up a typology based on the order of physical functions (typical plans for hospitals, hotels, schools, banks, etc.) which, however, has not produced any important formal results.[1]

Form is not predicated by function, and typology can be defined as neither form nor function. While form has been designated to issues of topology, how that form is built can be designated to typology as elements and systems.

1 Argan, Giulio Carlo. "On the Typology of Architecture." *Theorizing a New Agenda for Architecture: An Anthology of Architectural Theory 1965–1995*, edited by Kate Nesbitt, Princeton Architectural Press, New York, NY, 1996, pp. 242–246.

Rule of Engagement

In conversation with Christian Kerez

PRAUD   Let's start with a quick observation. Your work often gets analyzed, or commented on, from a structural standpoint. This could be an oversimplification as your work can be read as an expression of understanding "the rules of the game" as you named your GSD Kenzo Tange Lecture (2012). By "rules of the game," we can see your work as a manifestation of engaging the well-established rules from Modernism and inflicting them in order to produce a new space beyond modernism and into the contemporary. Would you say this is the case? Is there an anti-modern agenda?

CK   To give a bit of background, I was attending the university at the peak of post-modernism, and you had Charles Jenks as an influential theoretical figure, being one of the most published and theoretical thinkers of that time. It was very early for Swiss architecture, Jacques Herzog had just built his first house, the Blue House. And I remember, I was very suspicious against Postmodernism because, for me, it seemed to be very rhetorical or very much like a propagandistic mimic, making architecture new, even if it meant to go back to medieval times, or to classicism. It seemed to be a contradictory situation.
I showed a professor at the ETH the Blue House by Jacques, which for me, being an intern at that time, was already quite clear, that this is a new voice in Switzerland. He said that is without any interest, like a piece of art, you can do it only once. It is not a role model. Somehow, he hit the point. It is extraordinary work on the one hand, but it is not like a building by Mies or Le Corbusier that can serve as a role model for the next generation. I think we are still a bit on this kind of track.

If you want to do something new, it is not any more serving as a role model, but more as exceptional work. This can be even more off-track if you would consider your own work as something that is easy to recognize, that you can see right away, "Oh, this is a typical building by Christian Kerez," which positions you in a private cage with limited freedom. So I became interested in all this thinking about what is the evidence behind the project or what are the rules behind the project. Something that you don't have to explain my work with my autobiographical background. On the other hand, I'm aware that these rules are probably no more usable as role models, like the five points by Le Corbusier. So it is somehow driven by this desire to make something that is not private, but on the other hand, it's also aware that the time of role models is gone.

PRAUD   Your work, though, does seem to be building up a language that becomes somewhat universal to understanding this move beyond modernism, towards contemporary architecture, but of course it's very personal or signature from you in the way that you address specific elements in the building.

CK   Let's put it like that, of course, especially the early buildings, they have similarities, but the similarities are more like a miss-achievement. It's not something that I was looking for, but I couldn't just do it better. I think today, the projects are more different from one another. I remember the last lecture I gave in the United States, people were kind of confused, thinking, "what is this guy presenting or what is the message?" In that sense, it's much more where I want to go and what interests me, to have something that is evident in itself, without my interpretation or without a connection to authorship.

PRAUD   In that distanciation of authorship, I think your buildings start from a very pragmatic point of view, but then you end up working with the rules as a way to distort the elements. This somehow hints at a computational way of thinking in terms of understanding the essential parameters and how to play with them.

CK   Well I'm still very fascinated by modernism, and I'm totally fascinated by understanding the avant-garde, which I think was a specific historical situation that is gone and will never come back. In that sense, I truly believe it's still possible to make things that are new or that you haven't seen before, and that is an interest that I still want to keep you know that that could be related to modernist times, and that was also the kind of lack of satisfaction with Postmodernism. So many projects looked as though they were not new or different. That is maybe the commonality with the different postmodern projects. We just finished this year, House Okamura, we finished the pavilion in Dubai, the office building Lyon Confluence, at the same time with incidental space at the Venice Biennale. I mean just these four recently completed projects are so different from one another it's like they were done by four different companies or four different architects. But on the other hand, it's not random, it's not anything goes. I'm always looking for the evidence or the rules, in order to say, well, this is now maybe new, but it's also like a prototype even if it is a dysfunctional prototype. It's an intellectual prototype of how you could look at architecture in general. Maybe it will not politically or economically change the world as at least modernism pretended.

PRAUD   Similar to how you had skepticism towards postmodern architecture, we have a bit of cynical or critical thoughts on contemporary architecture. We see projects labeled as contemporary, but then upon further inspection, these projects are following the modern language and an embedded domino system with different façade treatments. With that perspective, we started to collect projects that try to break the rules of the modern language more directly. For your House With a Missing Column or the One Wall House, we cannot say that there is one language that explains both, but the attitude towards breaking the modern language is something that we can read from these houses as Contemporary projects.

CK   The question of what is contemporary architecture is really difficult because, on the one hand, you could say everything is possible, but if everything is possible, nothing is new. On the other hand, if it is just personal work, then it is not making any crucial remark about contemporary conditions, it is just the escape to a private refuge.

The House with One Wall was on the edge of what you could do as a young ambitious architect for a house for two families on the outskirts of Zurich. You could have made a crazy shape, but then, this is not in any way contemporary but a combination of different cliches.

So the idea was not to turn it into something completely different but to try to expose its true nature, a house with two apartments separated by a vertical wall. Of course, it would have also been possible, to separate in a horizontal section but then it would have not worked in terms of views, and plot surface. That was somehow a quick exercise, and the actual work came much later in trying to keep the innocence or purity of this concept.

But it is also then about how the folding of the wall all of a sudden is not anymore a formal act but also has a structural meaning, a functional programmatic meaning, a meaning in terms of the staircase. The form itself has no meaning and so the fascination for the project came only when we saw how difficult it is to implement all these meanings through the decision of having a dividing wall as the whole house.

The House with a Missing Column was quite different. It was a project that took a very long time and it seemed like an ongoing project somewhere in the office. At a certain moment, it became necessary to take certain parts of the program out because the site was just too small to have proper apartments. At first, it seemed to be like an automatic project from the 60s, with a main living room and attached cores for installations, elevator shaft, fire stairs. What made it somehow interesting is that it was not possible to make four cores to have a balanced structural system. It's like a chair where you have to cut one leg. At that point, the project started to interest me. It became clear that it needs beams that will be quite massive because there is this column missing.

And this brought to this otherwise very ordinary house an extraordinary scale and then at that moment, it became really exciting. Later on, we realized that these columns could go to the outside, like three cranes lifting the different platforms. That is how it then became conceptual and also specific.

That is one of the difficulties today. On the one hand, everything is possible, so even if you do something totally crazy it is boring because everybody can do it. On the other hand, there is no way back to commonplaces of the 60s or 70s because that's already done, and in a nicer way than what is possible today because these guys were not fighting with triple glazing and with separation of inside and outside and all these very difficult tasks that come from the pressures of the building industry, such as sustainability, for example.

PRAUD   In that sense, what were the outcomes of the Incidental Space and the Dubai Pavilion that you just completed? Because you can achieve different explorations in the pavilion scale rather than the building scale. What was the outcome in this relationship that you have to the rules and understanding this condition of having a pragmatic start followed by mutations?

CK   This question of rules is also in the end about the design process, not necessarily about the process as cultivation of formal language but as a kind of thinking into an abstract way on design.

The Venice project was about producing a space that you cannot easily recognize or associate with already existing spaces, a space that you cannot explain. This is somehow contradictory because if you have a rule, you can always explain it. The way how we worked on it was very much about having a continuous surface, with no interruptions. It is a surface project that would constantly change, having textures and a volumetric appearance. We did not want a collage where you could identify individual pieces.

PRAUD   Would you say that it's similar to how you just explained the One Wall House? One element works as structure, space, ornament. One element does it all, and in this case, it incorporates formal gestures that can mold into any formal aspect.

CK   Yes, you could somehow if you say the rule is always an
            abstraction of appearance. You could say, well, the goal
            is it's just the surface, then the whole project becomes
            extremely simple right?
            I remember then we had the question, how could this
            project make sense so that we get some financial support
            from the industry? We went to the industry and said look,
            this is the surface right. It's not very stable, but you
            can make it stable by increasing the complexity of the
            surface, which makes automatically these extremely thin
            elements stable. That was the moment when, at least, they
            were considering you know they might support.
            You could also say, well, there were these two rules:
            one is using the surface, and two, make it as complex as
            possible. The reason was of course not so much to change
            the building industry, but it was much more about the
            spatial experience of the extremely small space becoming
            scaleless. The project is very complex as geometry. You
            could also not produce such geometry on the computer. It
            was not a parametric design, even if everything is later
            on produced digitally, as it is also about the combination
            of dirty design and clean design with robots milling and
            three-dimensional printing, but we also had students
            working on physical models and casting them. So it was a
            combination of two totally different design approaches
            that normally are totally separated, like combining the
            Catholic Church and the Protestant church.

PRAUD   Many of your projects actually expose the structure. In
the Lyon Confluence project, the columns reduce in diameter at each
level as they go up. These are also exposed to the exterior as an
aesthetic move, which also reflects the nature of the structural
logic. In that sense, do you intentionally try to expose the
structure as part of the aesthetic gesture of your buildings?

CK   Maybe to come back to this question of rules and systems,
            if you have a system that is new, maybe it can have plenty
            of components that exist already, but the way how they are
            combined makes them new. This is for me a kind of a sublime

way of making something new. I'm always interested in this process of transforming how you can understand a system as new, through the old without becoming the prisoner of your own aesthetical preferences.

In Lyon, Herzog and de Meuron told each architect working on this plot, you have to use concrete per their masterplan. We initially worked on a classical idea of understanding how the building is different at the bottom than at the top. We were inspired to do this, not with decorative ornaments, but by layering systems, starting with wood, followed by concrete, and then by steel.

The Mayor and the developer didn't like that idea so much, so we decided we would work with concrete but we do it in a different way. We would layer techniques of forming concrete, starting with how maybe the Roman would work without any vibration needle, then we would use a conventional way, how you do it nowadays with a vibration needle and finally what is done very rarely basically for electrical flagpoles using fiber concrete turned in a steel tube.

We create something like a classical order. This may be nostalgic, but I think you can make new by interpreting this order through structural logic. You can innovate through the generic. You could also say this building looks like any other office building, and the only invention is how the elements relate to each other, not even the elements by themselves.

PRAUD Would you say also that these inflections are in a way, a strategy to test the form? You start with very pragmatic conditions of the site requiring so much FAR, BCR, and setbacks. If you follow these codes you end up with an ordinary allowable maximum volume. Then, through your interpretation of how elements relate to each other in a system, you end up with a deformation of the generic box. Like the Shenzhou high-rise, the columns become a canopy extending the form at the base.

CK Well, you have so many restraints that pose the question of whether architecture is still possible or if you can still make something different, that is not just the confirmation of the commonplace.

The form is something that does not interest me so much, yet somehow as an architect, I am interested in defining spaces and as a designer, I'm very interested in the question of systems and how the two relate to each other, thinking of how it works internally.

Somehow I wish there would be no boundaries, and each floor plan will be endless. This is of course the difficulty, dealing with boundaries but I don't want to consider a boundary as a limitation of thinking. This might be a reason why very often these forms are broken, and the form is more like a section. They are not glass boxes and similarly, we always see the continuation of the inside and the outside. Because it's the system that is endless that it just has a contemporary incidental boundary, even by coincidences.

PRAUD   Last question, as we mentioned in the beginning, we are investigating contemporary architecture and we wonder if there even is a language that we can say this is contemporary architecture. So in that sense, do you see your body of work as striving to find a contemporary language, perhaps as you mentioned at the beginning, that might serve as a role model? Or how do you see the contemporary scene?

CK   Every contemporary architecture wanted to prepare the future. It was never about the present. It was always about the question, what's next? What is there to come? Considering that we live in difficult times. It somehow looks a bit for me cynical, the language of contemporary architecture that is let's say so pretentious, that is looking for brand new.

Contemporary very quickly fall into the trap of becoming a kind of fashion. A lot of things that you could consider as contemporary are really nothing more than just satisfying a certain desire for fashion, new every year.

It is very difficult to prepare the future if it's so hard to believe in this future.

I have a simple answer to that. I basically would say my interest is in the intellectual understanding of architecture, more about how could you think things differently.

PRAUD   Would you say then that your architecture is about spatial efficiency in the way that each move that you make becomes a spatial logic, a structural logic, an effect, and ornamentation?

CK   In the work we produce, there is a certain restraint and a certain suspicion that is expressed and maybe that makes it contemporary.
We try to make something new but also no longer have the belief in a bright new future. I still share this desire for something new and different but maybe not anymore to serve as a role model, but just as an experience as such. It's a tricky question, to think about the contemporary. What's new nowadays, I really wonder. There are very few things that give me this feeling. For example, House Okamura I think maybe the building that is the most different in terms how it's thought from anything that I saw or experience so far, but it looks kind of old fashioned because it has these brick walls. But the experience is actually really quite strange.

PRAUD   That's is the struggle that we have also as well in putting this book, and thinking how do we define contemporary. Is there a common ground for discussion amongst other people in the field in a way that we can somehow categorize contemporary architecture?

175

FAÇADE DESIGN – FIVE POINTS OF ARCHITECTURE

Corbusier's Five Points of Architecture[2] re-structured the way architecture can be composed in a systematic way. The pilotis, first point, would allow the ground to be part of the public space while elevating the building. The structural grid frees the plan (second point). With a free plan, walls no longer need to work as structural elements and can be used freely to configure the interior space. The green roof, actually the fifth point, is maximizing the built form by providing additional use. The two remaining points, the free design of the façade and horizontal windows, should actually be considered as one point as they both refer to the possibility of separating the façade from any structural elements. Before modernism, load-bearing walls in the façade had to proportion windows based on vertical forces. The modern method of construction could divert forces away from the façade and down a column grid. The façade was now free to be designed at the will of the architect, and the long horizontal windows that evenly distribute light, providing a visual connection to the landscape, reinforced that separation of the façade as an ornament, and columns as structure.

2 Jeanneret, Pierre. "Five Points Towards a New Architecture." *Programs and Manifestoes on 20th-Century Architecture*, edited by Ulrich Conrads, MIT Press, Cambridge, MA, 1971, pp. 59–62.

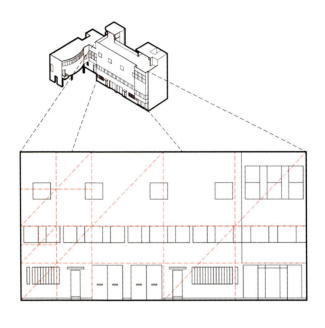

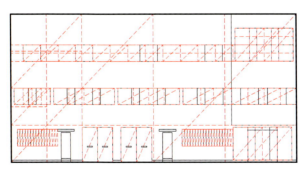

Villa la Roche,
Le Corbusier,
Paris, France. 1925

FAÇADE DESIGN – FIVE POINTS OF ARCHITECTURE

INTERCHANGEABLE FAÇADES

A façade that is independent of the structural system is almost a gift from Modernism. A new method of construction with reinforced concrete eliminates load-bearing walls from the façade, which allows for flexibility in the design of a façade without impacting overall structural decisions.

However, this gift was also a trap for contemporary architects. The unlimited possibilities for façade design are propelled by the array of accessible materials that are now available in the 21st century, from glass curtain walls to green walls, from rigid patterns to a parametric dynamic pattern, and from mass-produced walls to digitally fabricated custom walls. The trap is that regardless of using the most cutting-edge façade design, if the construction system that is hidden behind the façade is still a Modernist Dom-ino system, then the building will still be under the umbrella of Modernism. Hence, façade design would almost become similar to ornaments in Baroque Architecture, which hide the essence of the architectural system hidden by the superficial ornamentation.

179

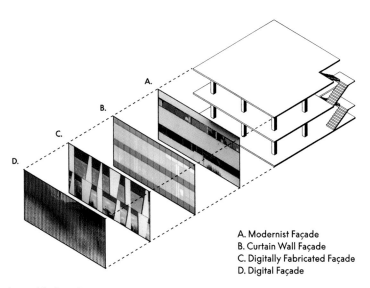

A. Modernist Façade
B. Curtain Wall Façade
C. Digitally Fabricated Façade
D. Digital Façade

Interchangable Façades

INTERCHANGEABLE FAÇADES

DECON-TEXTUAL

DECONSTRUCTIVIST ARCHITECTURE[3] focuses on seven international architects whose recent work marks the emergence of a new sensibility in architecture. The architects recognize the imperfectability of the modern world and seek to address, in Johnson's words, the "pleasures of unease." Obsessed with diagonals, arcs, and warped planes, they intentionally violate the cubes and right angles of modernism. Their projects continue the experimentation with structure initiated by the Russian Constructivists, but the goal of perfection of the 1920s is subverted. The traditional virtues of harmony, unity, and clarity are displaced by disharmony, fracturing, and mystery. The exhibition includes drawings, models, and site plans for recent projects by Coop Himmelblau, Peter Eisenman, Frank Gehry, Zaha M. Hadid, Rem Koolhaas, Daniel Libeskind, and Bernard Tschumi (list of projects attached). Their works are preceded by an Introductory section of Constructivist paintings and sculptures drawn from the Museum's collection.

(MOMA Press Release. March 1988)[4]

3 Johnson, Philip, and Mark Wigley. *Deconstructivist Architecture*. Museum of Modern Art, New York, NY, 1988.
4 "DECONSTRUCTIVIST ARCHITECTURE." *https://www.moma.org/Calendar/ Exhibitions/1813*, MoMA, Mar. 1988, https://assets.moma.org/documents/moma_press-release_327505.pdf. Accessed 15 Feb. 2022.

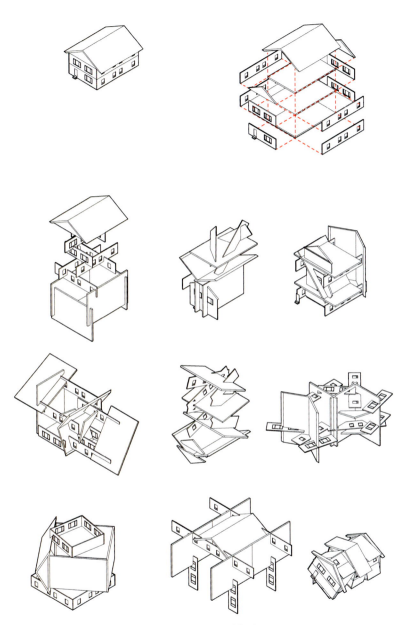

Deconstructing building elements to then reassemble the same elements in a different configuration.

DECON-TEXTUAL

SEPARATION OF ROLES BY ELEMENTS

The elements of modernism have been independently used for the purpose of providing structure, an expression of aesthetics, or to formalize a space. For modernism based on the five points by Le Corbusier, columns provide support, while walls define a space, and the façade is designed independently for expression and ornamentation. Yet, these elements could cross over in roles blending roles between elements and systems. The floor could become spatial, a façade could be structural, a column could be ornamental.

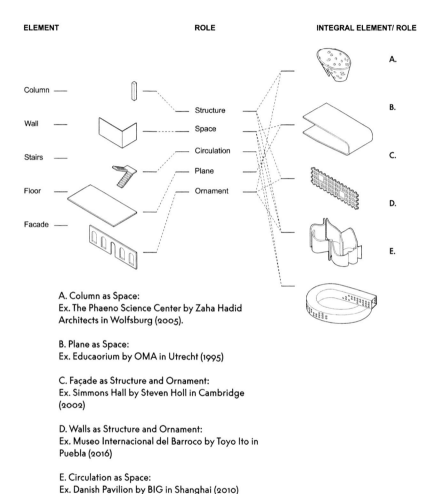

A. Column as Space:
Ex. The Phaeno Science Center by Zaha Hadid Architects in Wolfsburg (2005).

B. Plane as Space:
Ex. Educaorium by OMA in Utrecht (1995)

C. Façade as Structure and Ornament:
Ex. Simmons Hall by Steven Holl in Cambridge (2002)

D. Walls as Structure and Ornament:
Ex. Museo Internacional del Barroco by Toyo Ito in Puebla (2016)

E. Circulation as Space:
Ex. Danish Pavilion by BIG in Shanghai (2010)

**Elements or Modernism,
Diagram of roles of elements.**

SEPARATION OF ROLES BY ELEMENTS

BEYOND MODERNISM

Through the intermixing of roles from the modernist elements, as defined by the maison Dom-ino (slabs, columns, and stairs), new strategies for space making could be generated by transforming these elements through oppositions to the domino model. For example, the façade which is non-structural in the domino system could become the major structural element while also serving an ornamental function. Slabs could be inflected to become circulation or space. Columns could become spatial by increasing their perimeters and being able to hold a program inside of them.

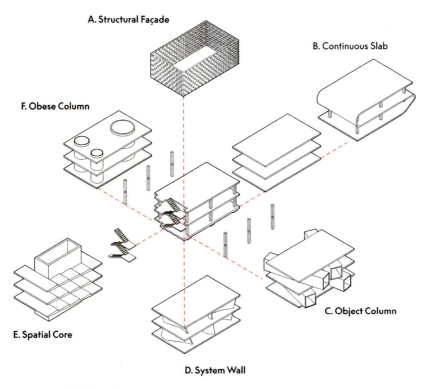

Mutations of Modern System

BEYOND MODERNISM

IN-TENSION

By borrowing structural methods from civil engineering, some architects pushed the envelope of architectural structures mimicking engineered elements. While many architects are intrigued by the concept of architecture that floats in an anti-gravity state, they struggle from restrictions and limitations in the length of span and cantilever. Civil engineers, on the other hand, take a pragmatic, simple, and cost-effective approach to solve the problem of spanning structures with minimum elements. Wire suspension bridges, for example, have existed for over a century, dating back to Joseph Chaley's Grand Pont Suspendu in Fribourg, from 1834. These techniques have been known to architects as well, yet are often overseen as a Civil Engineering agenda outside of the realm of architecture. João Filgueiras Lima demonstrated otherwise with the Centro de Exposições do Centro Administrativo da Bahia where a mass 52 m long by 9 m wide is suspended 5 m off the ground while balancing from the center with suspension cables. Both the Federal Reserve Bank engineered by LERA in Minneapolis and the proposal by Louis Kahn for the Palazzo dei Congressi in Venice use a suspension bridge system with catenaries.

During the 1950s and 1960s, Oscar Niemeyer worked on a series of projects that appeared to be exoskeletons guarding a building. Projects like the Palácio da Alvorada (1958) or the more evolved Sede Mondadori (1968) demonstrated a manipulation of the engineering system as elements of expression. Not until the Fabbrica Automazione Trasporti e Affini (FATA) would Niemeyer really demonstrate a new capacity for the engineering and architecture language to fuse. The FATA headquarters works like a land bridge, suspending a box through a rhythm of hanging columns from a pretensed beam with cantilevers of 31 m. The prowess of floating an entire building was achieved again in 2010 with the inauguration of the Tiradentes Palace where Niemeyer would float a four-story building. Smaller projects like the Niemeyer Museum or his Serpentine Pavilion also made use of bridging systems to perform an integral idea of space.

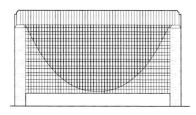

FEDERAL RESERVE BANK
Gunnar Birkerts
Minneapolis, USA. 1973

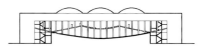

PALAZZO DEI CONGRESSI
Louis Kahn
Venice, Italy. 1972

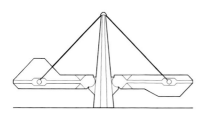

CENTRO DE EXPOSIÇÕES DO CENTRO ADMINISTRATIVO DA BAHIA
João Filgueiras Lima
Bahia, Brazil. 1974

SERPENTINE PAVILION
Oscar Niemeyer
London, UK. 2003

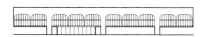

FATA HEADQUARTERS
Oscar Niemeyer
Turin, Italy. 1975

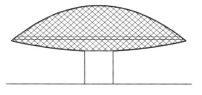

OSCAR NEIMEYER MUSEUM
Oscar Niemeyer
Curitiba, Brazil. 2002

Elevations for six different projects that use suspension structures.

IN-TENSION

FAÇADE

There are four different ways of understanding the expression of structure with relation to a façade.

1. Structural Aesthetic: the structural system forms the overall aesthetic of an architectural piece. The aesthetics of architecture derives directly from the beauty of the structural form.

2. The Function of Façade: as a homage to the Function of Ornament by Farshid Moussavi, the façade has a structural system independent from the rest of the building. Having two structural systems may be a redundancy, yet it liberates the design plasticity of the façade from the main structure of the building.

3. Structural Façade: the façade and its elements are part of the structural system of the whole building. Before the Domino system, the façade was not independent of the building structure, hence the façade would have to work as a load-bearing system of walls that served the overall structural system. Originally deriving from the stone masonry construction method, it is often used with steel or concrete construction.

4. The System of Expression: the façade system goes beyond the logic of structure itself. Unlike the other three categories that are more bound to structural decisions, the System of Expression is a hybrid solution between architectural aesthetic and a structural system. It may not be so obvious that what is seen on the façade is a structural system that holds the building because of its expressional values that may not follow pragmatic structural decisions directly, yet it is integral for the structural, aesthetics, and spatial composition.

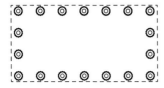

A. Structural Aesthetics:
Ex. The Parthenon in Athens (438 BC)

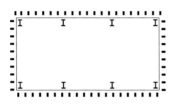

B. The Function of Façade:
Ex. Seagram Building in New York by Mies van der Rohe (1958)

C. Structural Façade:
Ex. Palazzo di Medici in Florence by Michelozzo di Bartolomeo (1444-1484)

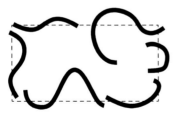

D. System of Expression:
Ex. Christian Dior Flagship Store in Seoul by Christian de Portzamparc (2015)

FAÇADE

TUBE FRAME

Fazlur Kahn's first project at SOM consisted of a 43-story building in Chicago where he introduced the first tube structure for skyscrapers.[5] The revolutionary engineering contribution came from the design of a structural façade that would support the building in order to maximize the interior space. More than an advancement in structural engineering, it would reemphasize the façade as the hierarchical element that should produce an architectural effect in parallel to its structural role.

5 Mortice, Zach, et al. "Fazlur Khan Converged Engineering, Architecture at the Top of the World." *Redshift EN*, 11 Nov. 2020, https://redshift.autodesk.com/fazlur-khan/.

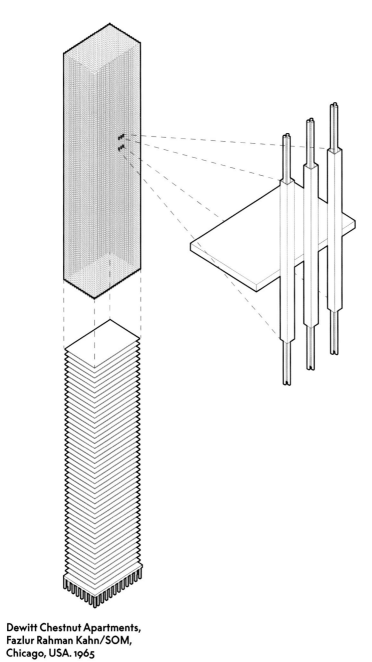

Dewitt Chestnut Apartments,
Fazlur Rahman Kahn/SOM,
Chicago, USA. 1965

TUBE FRAME

STRUCTURAL EFFECT

In opposition to the modernist tendencies to free the façade, Steven Holl's Simmons Hall at MIT uses the façade as an integral part of the building form, system, and aesthetics. The precast concrete grid creates a thick façade wall reminiscent of a masonry system of support where windows are limited in size for structural stability. In this case, the windows are not punched windows but rather a repetition of the waffle grid system that produces a trompe l'oeil on the scale of the building. At the same time, the coloring of the windows comes from the structural analysis of the system so that the building is a literal representation of its own structural logic.

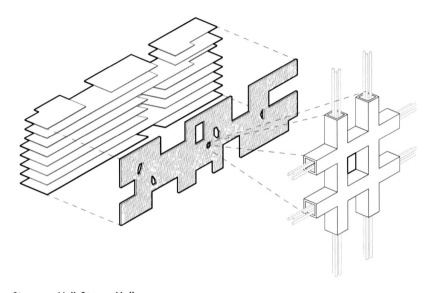

Simmons Hall, Steven Holl,
Cambridge,
USA. 2002

STRUCTURAL EFFECT

MATERIAL LOGIC

What at first instance seems to be an ornamental pattern is a deceptive structural one. A metal honeycomb material forms an orthogonal tunnel structure. The honeycomb material has structural properties for spanning horizontally, yet it is weaker and collapsible when tilted on its side and used for compression. Just like in the case of a honeycomb cardboard, adding a layer of paper on either side makes the cardboard stand. In the Brugge pavilion, the metal ovals act like the paper on the honeycomb cardboard. All the material in this form is optimized as a structural logic while performing also as an ornament for the production of a spatial effect.

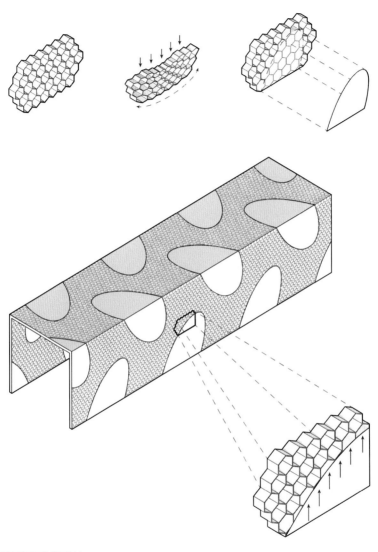

BRUGGE PAVILION
Toyo Ito
Brugge, Belgium. 2002
A honecomb pattern collapses when used
vertically, requiring additional surface support.
This produces the sturctural pattern for the pavilion.

MATERIAL LOGIC

STRUCTURAL ORNAMENT

There is a distinction to be made between structural façade and structural ornament as a façade. In a building like TOD's Omotesando Building by Toyo Ito, the façade is achieving all the structural needs for the building, liberating the interior space of the columns. This is also the strategy on the modernist Twin Towers which looked at maximizing the office space through a structural façade. In this case, the structure also abstracts the pattern of trees in order to become an ornamental architectural effect as well as a system.

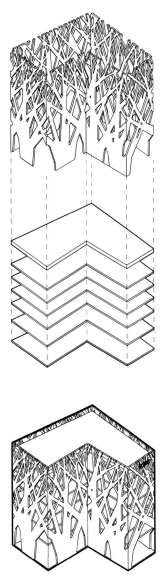

TOD's Omotesando Building,
Toyo Ito,
Tokyo, Japan. 2004

STRUCTURAL ORNAMENT

HOLISTIC ORNAMENT

Adopted by the revolutions in digital technology, Fazlur Kahn's structural tube was envisioned as an ornamental structural element that would not only free the interior but it would also provide sectional variance. Tested in concrete, its plasticity and compression strength allow it to be molded and patterned independently from any interior condition, as is the case for O-14 by RUR.

> "The concrete shell of O-14 provides an efficient structural exoskeleton that frees the core from the burden of lateral forces and creates highly efficient, column-free open spaces in the building's interior. The exoskeleton of O-14 becomes the primary vertical and lateral structure for the building, allowing the column-free office slabs to span between it and the minimal core."[6]

The same concept is tested in a period of five years with Torre Glories in Barcelona by Jean Nouvel, the Mikimoto Building in Tokyo by Toyo Ito, O-14 in Dubai by RUR (as previously stated), Sia Aoyama Building in Tokyo by Jun Aoki, and the Urban Hive in Seoul by Archium. This repetition of the strategy shows the versatility of the system to produce spatial variations in a vertical configuration.

6 "O-14." *Reiser+Umemoto, RUR Architecture DPC*, https://www.reiser-umemoto.com/selected-projects/o-14.

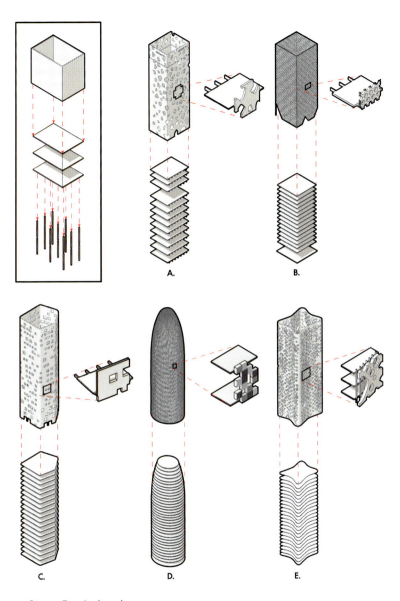

A. Mikimoto Ginza 2, Toyo Ito (2005)
B. Urban Hive, Archium (2008)
C. SIA Aoyama Building, Jun Aoki (2008)
D. Torre Glòries, Jean Nouvel (2004)
E. O-14, RUR (2010)

Diagrams of five structural tube projects.

HOLISTIC ORNAMENT

HYPERBOLIC PARABOLOIDS

As an engineer, Eladio Dieste tested the limits of certain construction systems through the efficiency of materials.

> "A particular innovation was his Gaussian vault, a thin-shell structure for roofs in single-thickness brick, that derives its stiffness and strength from a double curvature catenary arch form that resists buckling failure."[7]

Much like Felix Candela's Los Manantiales from 1958, the use of hyperbolic paraboloids allows for the form to work as a structural system.

7 Pedreschi, R, Theodossopoulos, D, *ICE Proceedings, Structures and Buildings*, Vol 160, Issue 1, pp. 3–11.

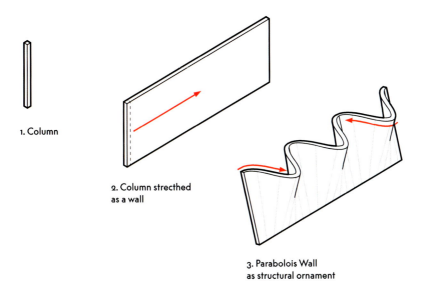

1. Column
2. Column strecthed as a wall
3. Parabolois Wall as structural ornament

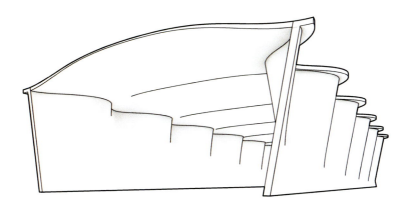

Iglesia Del Cristo Obrero,
Eladio Dieste,
Atlántida, Uruguay. 1952

HYPERBOLIC PARABOLOIDS

LOFTING

Commissioned in 1965, the Pagoda building demonstrated the plasticity of form manipulation through precast concrete. The twisting floor plates at 45 degrees were connected through parabolic walls that enforced the visual effect of rotation. Aside from the aesthetic order achieved through this deformation, the building showed a break from a traditional extrusion logic to a lofting surface logic achievable through new construction technology that deviated from modernist tendencies.

203

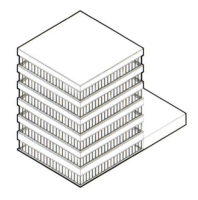 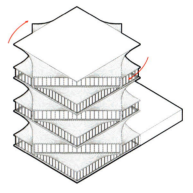

La Pagoda,
Miguel Fisac,
Madrid, Spain. 1970

LOFTING

WALL SPACING

NARRATOR: Please begin by walking around the outside of Torqued Ellipse IV. Its steel surface has been sandblasted leaving a layer of rust.

When Richard Serra first became interested in bending plates of steel over 25 years ago, he felt he'd had little experience with large-scale curved surfaces.

RICHARD SERRA: I realized that there wasn't a large vocabulary of building with curvilinear forms, particularly in a city that's made up of right angles. The only curvature building I can think of any note in the city at that time was Frank Lloyd Wright's Guggenheim Museum. And I wanted to build something that would inform my experience.

NARRATOR: Walking around his curved pieces, Serra realized that the experience of the outside of a curve was very different from the experience within it.

RICHARD SERRA: If you walk around the curve, you don't know how it's going to round. It seems continuous and never ending. But the concave side like a cave, reveals itself in its entirety. You know what the form is.[8]

8 "Richard Serra. Torqued Ellipse IV. 1998: Moma." *The Museum of Modern Art*, https://www.moma.org/audio/playlist/236/3051.

Torqued ellipses,
Richard Serra, 1997

WALL SPACING

FOUR WALLS

The following is from the Gebhard Decaspei structural aspects.
The engineer's report[9]

> The architectural concept called for the inside of the building to be separated from the external façade by 120 mm of thermal insulation without erecting a second load-bearing wall to support the floor slabs. This in turn called for an optimum engineering solution in order to transfer the support reactions from the walls and floors to the external façade. The answer was to use high-strength double shear studs.
>
> At ground floor level the two walls to the left and right of the stairs are the primary structural elements supporting the first floor. The inner walls of the first and second floors are the structural elements for the floor and roof above respectively. The interaction with the floor and roof slabs (walls as webs, slabs as flanges) is taken into account. All the support reactions are transferred as the wall junctions transverse to the external walls. Double shear studs, one above the other, were incorporated in the façade at these junctions. The number of shear studs required depends on the load bearing capacity of a single stud.
>
> In order to eliminate the deflection of the unsupported slab edges (spans between 8.0 and 10.0 m) along the façade, additional support points with shear studs were incorporated in the centre of each slab edge span and at the corners of the façade.
>
> Special attention had to be given to transferring the shear forces at the shear studs. The thermal insulation had to be reduced to 50 mm around the shear studs; however, this was acceptable in terms of the thermal requirements. In order to prevent – as far as possible – the formation of cracks in the external walls, particularly around the long windows, considerable additional longitudinal reinforcement was fitted in the areas at risk. The structural analysis of this new building represented a real challenge for the engineer.

9 Hesson, Robert. "Valerio Olgiati - Frame Construction." *Northern Architecture*, 7 Jan. 2022, https://www.northernarchitecture.us/frame-construction/valerio-olgiati.html.

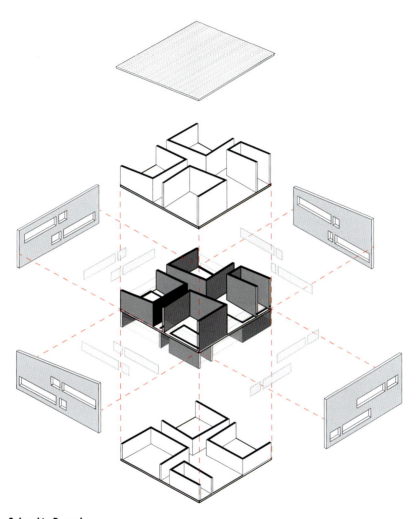

School in Paspels,
Valerio Olgiati,
Paspels, Switzerland. 1998

FOUR WALLS

ONE WALL

"...the folding of the wall all of a sudden is not anymore a formal act but also has a structural meaning, a functional programmatic meaning, a meaning in terms of the staircase. The form itself has no meaning and so the fascination for the project came only when we saw how difficult it is to implement all these meanings through the decision of having a dividing wall as the whole house."[10]

10 From "In Conversation with Christian Kerez."

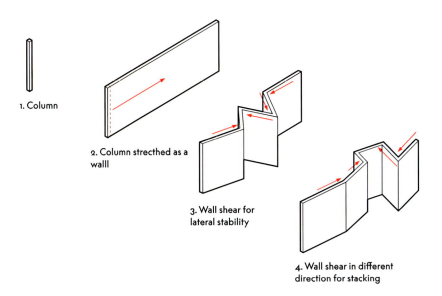

1. Column
2. Column stretched as a walll
3. Wall shear for lateral stability
4. Wall shear in different direction for stacking

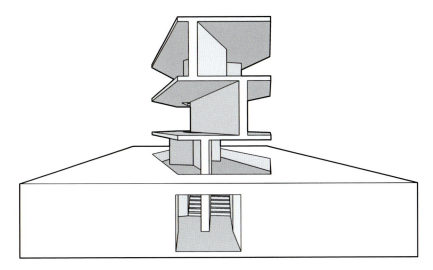

House with One Wall,
Christian Kerez,
Zurich, Switzerland. 2007

ONE WALL

FLUID SURFACE

Sited in the Millennium Park of Chicago, this temporary pavilion serves almost as a direct reference to the Farnsworth House, an iconic international style modern building in the suburbs of Chicago. Mies' masterpiece would frame nature between two elevated horizontal planes that were supported by exterior columns. The interior of the house was a universal space, absent of rooms, that would only take form through its furniture and non-structural room partitions, allowing for a fluid transition from space to space. For the Burnham Pavilion, the two horizontal planes compose the boundary of space. The columns and partitions are missing from this diagram. Instead, the upper slab melts to a catenary in three points producing a structural balance and a fluid continuation of the in-between space. The plane is partitioned through a Single Surface operation that works as structure, ornament, and space.

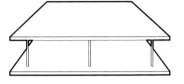
1. Modern frame

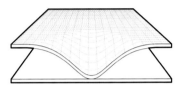
2. Slab as structure

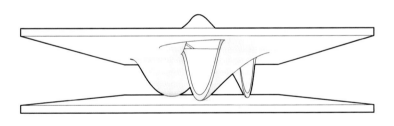

Burnham Pavilion,
UN Studio,
Chicago, USA. 2009

FLUID SURFACE

FLUID WALLS

In 2006, Toyo Ito was given a commission to design the new Berkeley Art Museum in California, which initiated an exploration by Ito on the use of the wall as the primary element and system. Following a grid, the walls are bent at a specific corner in order to create structural moment connections, as well as spatial and visual connections. Although the project was not constructed, the system was tested a decade later with the Museo Internacional del Barroco. For this museum, the slabs take a lesser role and the walls are the predominant compositional elements. The walls form a series of chambers that rotate as the walls also twist on their ends for structural stability. This represents a break in the system, wherein the Berkeley Museum there was a direct reference to the modernist slab, the Museo del Barroco becomes an additive system on its own.

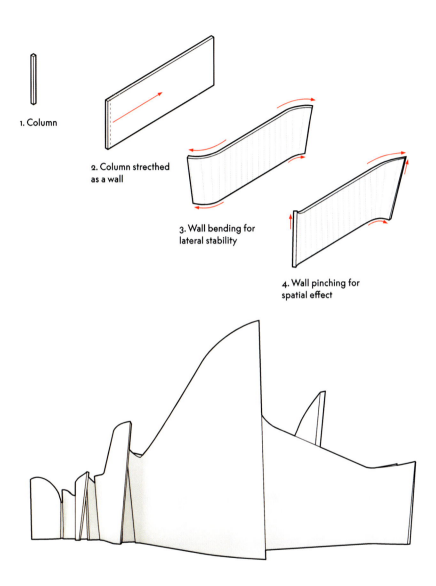

1. Column
2. Column strecthed as a wall
3. Wall bending for lateral stability
4. Wall pinching for spatial effect

Museo Internacional Del Barroco,
Toyo Ito,
Puebla, Mexico. 2016

FLUID WALLS

DOM-INO SLAB

This winning entry competition by OMA for the Jussie – Two Libraries is iconically represented through an image of a large-scale model that is backlit to emphasize the silhouette reading of a column grid and slab system. The lack of façade in the model or the transparent core is unimportant, as this is a direct study on the inflection of the slab in order to produce a continuous promenade rather than a stacking of floor plates. As an insertion to the Edouard Albert's Jussieu campus, this library must consider the open circulation system of the campus. The continuous slab that the library proposes extends the campus circulation as a micro-city inside the building. Program is arranged as an urban vertical experience. This model breaks the monotony of the modernist slab system and radically changes the concept of the floor as a static absolute boundary to a ground that can achieve circulation, program, and space.

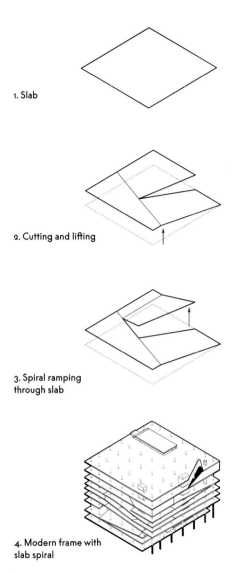

1. Slab
2. Cutting and lifting
3. Spiral ramping through slab
4. Modern frame with slab spiral

Jussieu – Two libraries,
OMA, Paris,
France. 1992.

DOM_INO SLAB

CONTINUOUS SLAB

As a way to create a fluid sequence of programs, two planes fold bringing the ground into the building. The folded slab is pierced with a column grid accentuating this deviation from the modernist norm. The moment of bending the slab to fold the space becomes the reception to the auditorium and the interior space of tension where the slab is exposed outside of its elemental capacities.

217

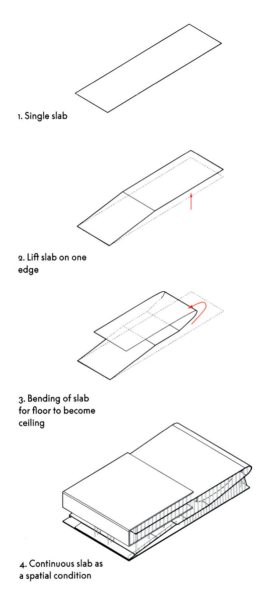

1. Single slab

2. Lift slab on one edge

3. Bending of slab for floor to become ceiling

4. Continuous slab as a spatial condition

**Educatorium,
OMA,
Utrecht, The Netherlands. 1995.**

CONTINUOUS SLAB

SINGLE SURFACE

The Luxor Theater competition from 1996 introduces a new problem for the production of architectural variance through a Single Surface. The abstraction of a red carpet rolling all the way to the theater and curling to form the balconies is intended to unify the public and eliminate hierarchies of users. The manipulation of a single architectural element provides a space for all the required programs through a Single Surface gesture.

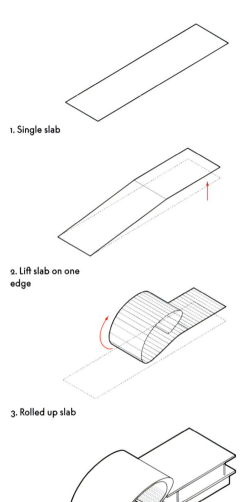

1. Single slab
2. Lift slab on one edge
3. Rolled up slab
4. Space as a single surface

Luxor Theatre,
OMA,
Rotterdam, The Netherlands. 1996.

SINGLE SURFACE

RIBBON

One of the more rigorous studies on the Single Surface project evolved as a series of proposals undertaken by Diller, Scofidio + Renfro, after their winning scheme for the Eyebeam Museum in New York. The Single Surface has presented a problem of duality between sides for services and for programs. The Eyebeam Museum proposal deals with the problem as a double ribbon configuration with an in-between space for services and would allow for spaces of encounter at split levels (later tested at the Center for Creative Arts in 2007). In 2003 the Institute of Contemporary Arts in Boston allowed for the ribbon concept to be tested in construction.

"The site is bound on two sides by the Harbor Walk, a 47-mile public walkway. The Harborwalk is used as a civic surface that extends up to form the public grandstand, flattens into the theater stage, and wraps the surfaces of the theater extending into a horizontal tray that holds the gallery and shelters the grandstand."[11]

The ICA incorporates the ground as an essential compositional tool for physically manifesting publicness in the spatial order. This becomes the general strategy on the following explorations like the Museum of Image and Sound commissioned in 2009.

"The building is conceived as an extension of that boulevard, stretched vertically into the museum. The 'Vertical Boulevard' gestures toward inclusiveness: it gently traverses indoor and outdoor spaces and branches to make galleries, education programs, spaces of public leisure and entertainment."

The commission for the Roy and Diana Vagelos Education Center in 2010 proposes a "vertical study cascade" in a 14-story building that merges social spaces and academic spaces. Limited by the constraints of the site, the vertical connections are achieved through ribbon slab manipulations.

11 "Institute of Contemporary Art." *DS+R*, https://dsrny.com/project/institute-of-contemporary-art?index=false§ion=projects.

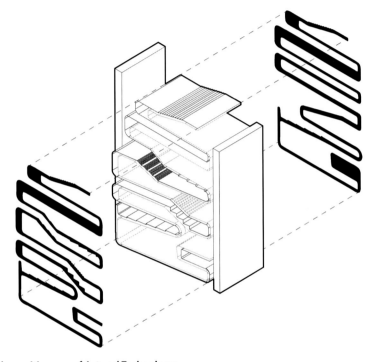

Eyebeam Museum of Art and Technology,
DS+R,
New York, USA. 2002

RIBBON

COLUMN EXPRESSION

This project is categorized as one of the few buildings by Lucio Costa in Brasilia. Despite masterplanning the city, few buildings are attributed to him. As a TV tower infrastructure project, Costa makes the most out of the minimum required elements by sculpting three mega columns that hold an observation deck as well as the tower above. This utilitarian infrastructure is transformed into an architectural spatial object through the plasticity of deforming its structural elements.

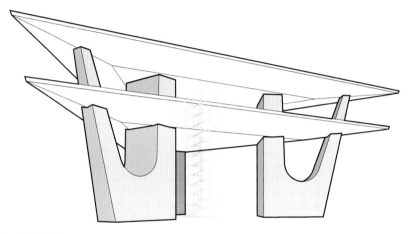

Brasilia TV Tower,
Lúcio Costa,
Brasília, Brazil. 1967

COLUMN EXPRESSION

COLUMN FRAME

Commissioned to build a museum that wouldn't obstruct the view on the site, Lina Bobardi separated the programs and massing of the museum by burying half of the massing and floating the other half. By separating the massing into two volumes, a plaza is created at ground level as the in-between space, as the roof of the buried mass and covered by the floating mass. Conceptually, the upper mass must float above the ground to create the covered plaza and entry to the building with minimum obstructions both visual and spatial. Structurally, in order to reduce the number of elements that would obstruct the plaza, two massive structural frames wrap around the entire upper mass.

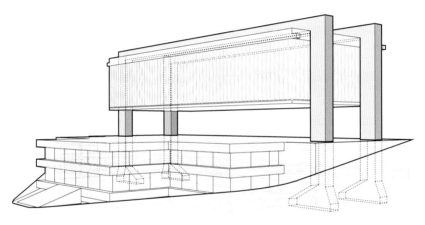

MASP,
Lina Bo Bardi,
São Paulo, Brazil. 1968

COLUMN FRAME

STRAPPING COLUMN

As part of Tange's agenda for promoting metabolism as an architectural strategy for redevelopment, the Tokyo Project of 1960 expanded the city along an axis from central Tokyo and across Tokyo Bay. The plan called for the redevelopment of Tsukiji, and Tange proposed the Tsukiji Redevelopment plan of 1964, where the Dentsu Headquarters would take form. His original proposal for the headquarters building envisioned a metabolism approach for growing the city vertically while liberating the ground. Four mega columns would strap around horizontal bar buildings, lifting them off the ground, and freeing the ground for public use. Through the repetition of these columns, the city could continue to expand using the air rights as a three-dimensional city.

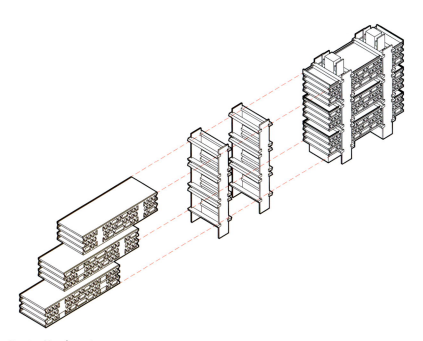

Dentsu Headquarters,
Kenzo Tange,
Tokyo, Japan. 1967

STRAPPING COLUMN

TABLE COLUMN

Similar to a table structure, the Edo Tokyo Museum is lifted from the ground by four cores that stabilize a cantilevered volume producing an open covered plaza. The four legs were built first to hold the cantilevered mass, which spanned 36 m on each side. Its elevation is an abstraction of a traditional rice storehouse, traditionally elevated off the ground with multiple columns that served as a table to hold the house above. This museum abstracts that condition by blending the concept of the table and house as one single structural element.

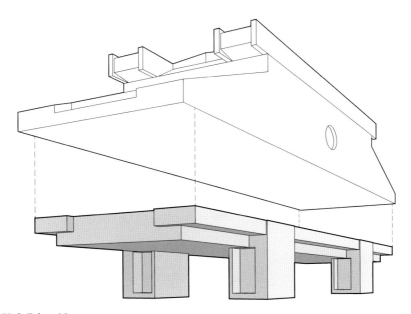

EDO-Tokyo Museum,
Kiyonori Kikutake,
Tokyo, Japan. 1993

TABLE COLUMN

TABLES

A collection of tables with rice bowls and other dishes are stacked vertically following a central axis. They are not arranged necessarily in a perfectly symmetrical composition. Each table is different in style, and the dishes are placed randomly on top of each table. Each table is structurally autonomous, hence the tables could also have been stacked randomly with a varying vertical axis. This installation by Choi Jeong-hwa also serves as a reference for an architectural structural system. The table surface is structural and can hold a load at any location along its surface. A structural slab works the same way. Columns and slabs do not have to align vertically as long as the slab can transfer the load. A structural slab would allow for rooms to be placed anywhere like the dishes on the table.

A Feast of Flower,
Choi Jeonghwa,
Seoul, Korea. 2015

TABLES

SPATIAL COLUMN

> "The simplest intentions of focusing on plates (floors), tubes (columns), and skin (façade/exterior walls) allows for a poetic and visually intriguing design, as well as a complex system of activities and informational systems."[12]

The simplicity in the concept evokes a drastic paradigm shift at the turn of the century, one as a typological exploration. The formal aspect of the building is not trying to achieve anything more than a maximum volume on-site. The elements used by the architect to describe the building are plates, tubes, and skin (slab, column, and façade). Although the columns follow a grid, and the intent is to have a free plan, the columns are thickened in sections in order to house services and produce an unobstructed floor plan. The grid of spatial columns is more than just a structural system; it is a spatial organizational system.

12 Sveiven, Megan. "Ad Classics: Sendai Mediatheque / Toyo Ito & Associates." *ArchDaily*, ArchDaily, 9 Mar. 2011, https://www.archdaily.com/118627/ad-classics-sendai-mediatheque-toyo-ito.

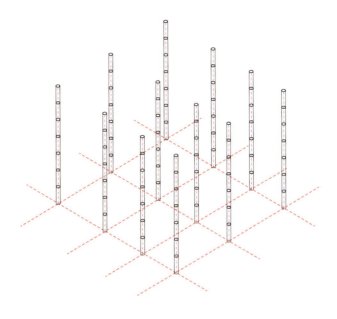

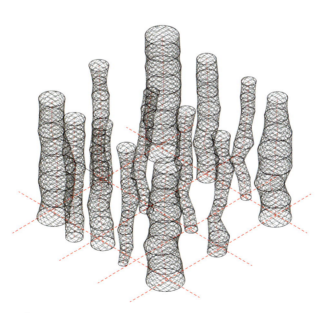

Sendai Mediatheque,
Toyo Ito,
Sendai, Japan. 2001

SPATIAL COLUMN

PROGRAMMABLE COLUMN

"The building must be considered as a single entity, impossible to dismantle, or to treat any one part of it in isolation: even the vertical 'cones', which are the main support for the building, also depend on the slab for restraint. This could only be achieved through the use of the latest three-dimensional modelling technology, carving a path for future designs."[13]

As described by the engineers at AKT, the cone formations are essential not only for the structural support for the mass above but also for the spatial logic. By allowing for the cones to be programmatic, it produces a covered plaza as an entry to the project. Services such as ticketing and information would occur at this ground level while the main program resides on the elevated mass.

13 "Phæno Science Centre." *AKT II*, 2 Sept. 2021, https://www.akt-uk.com/projects/phaeno-science-centre/.

235

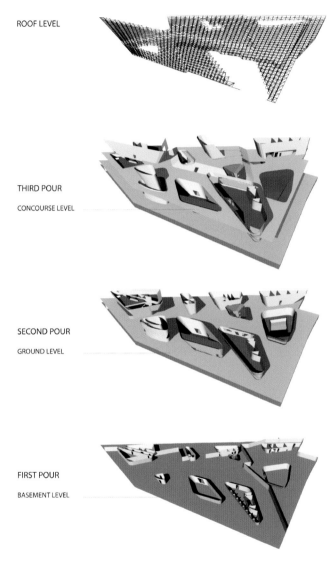

Phaeno Science Centre,
Zaha Hadid,
Wolfsburg, Germany. 2005

PROGRAMMABLE COLUMN

ROOM COLUMN

Divided into four masses, the church was designed to be built in sections. The progress of construction depended on the fundraising efforts by the community; hence, each volume is intended to be built independently of the others. The volumes are composed of room columns that house services such as restrooms or meditation spaces. This allows for an additive process of forming the building at various stages while allowing each element to be autonomous, yet form a total composition when completed.

237

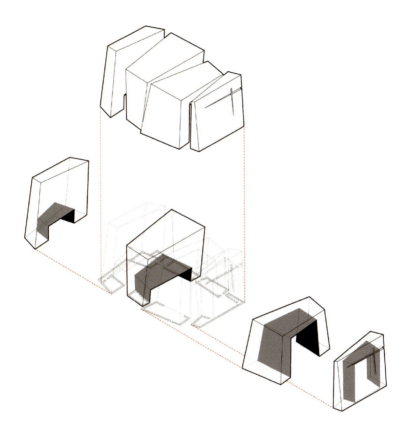

Fernando Menis,
Tenerife, Spain. 2008

ROOM COLUMN

FLAT COLUMN

Systems of columns and beams are dependent on bracing to resist lateral shear forces. These are resolved with shear walls or cross bracing. In this instance, a flat column system achieves both. Their apparent randomness and variation actually help to stabilize the structure, working as both support and ornament.

239

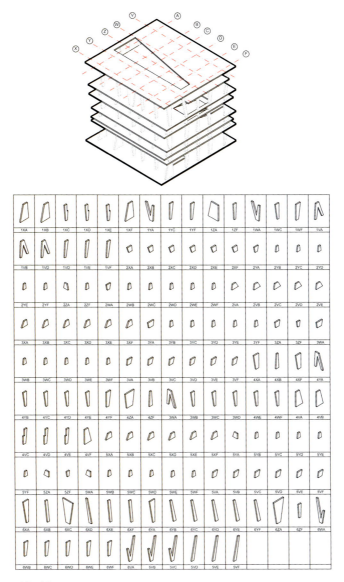

Herzog and De Meuron,
1111 Lincoln Road,
Miami, USA. 2010

FLAT COLUMN

MODULAR SLAB COLUMN

What appears to be a building that bends its slabs to produce a Single Surface space is actually a composition of five variations of column-slab modules. The arranged placement for the different modules produces the building with different opposing effects of continuity and separations.

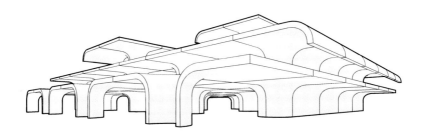

Daum Headquarters,
Mass Studies,
Jeju, Korea. 2012

MODULAR SLAB COLUMN

OBJECT COLUMN

This simple storefront installation stacks glass bases and glass shelves. The shelves align vertically and are supported by glass bases that are placed randomly at each level of the shelves. The bases are acting as "columns" while the glass shelves are "slabs." Similar to the table concept, the slab is structural and can hold a load at any point. Different from the table, it does not have a clear set of columns that hold it up. Instead, the objects on the shelves are the columns themselves. These are object columns. The objects are self-standing and spatial. They work as structures as well as containers, which in architecture could be programmatic.

Bases and glass shelves

OBJECT COLUMN

SKEWER CORE

Built as an extension to the SC Johnson Administration building, the research tower supplies unobstructed floors by cantilevering from a central core. Alternating between circular mezzanines and full square floor plates, double heights are achieved, granting vertical visual connections. Similar to a skewer, the core represents the primary organizer, bundling all the services while layering the floor plates. In section, each floor plate tapers in thickness from the core to the edge expressing the diminishing need for materials and support as it spans out. As a chemical research facility, the core not only consists of stairs, elevator, toilet, and shafts for air supply and exhaust, but also supports specialized lab requirements for compressed air, nitrogen, carbon dioxide, and steam.

245

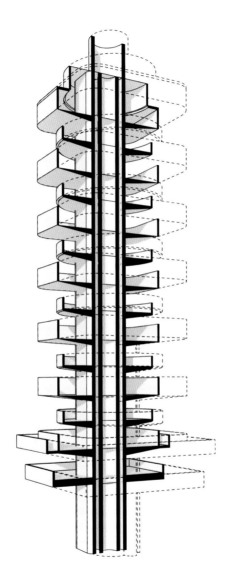

SC Johnson Wax Research Tower,
Frank Lloyd Wright,
Racine, USA. 1950

SKEWER CORE

STRETCHING CORE

Described as an analogy of a tree trunk holding its branches out, the Price Tower building cantilevers its floor plates from a branched core, giving the core the primary role of structure and spatial organizer. Wright's intention was to use the core not only for its pragmatic functional use but also to perform a spatial effect. The core organizes the floor plates into four quadrants which allow the building to introduce a new model of vertical mix-use. Each floor could be occupied by three offices and one residential unit.

247

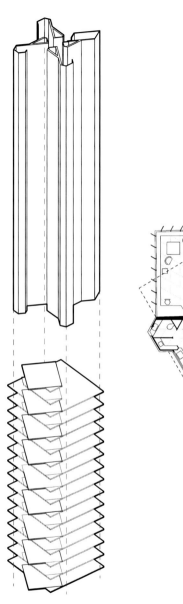
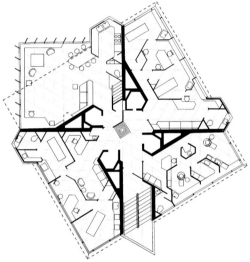

Price Tower,
Frank Lloyd Wright,
Bartlesville, USA. 1956
Core extruding to separate the
building in quadrants.

STRETCHING CORE

SIAMESE CORE

In order to maximize the office space, the Inland Steel Building makes two moves. First, all the structural steel columns are moved to the perimeter of a 19-story office building. Second, it consolidates the services (elevators, electrical and telephone lines, stairwells, risers, and restrooms) into a single 25-story structure next to the office tower. Almost like Siamese twins, the service tower and office tower stand side by side with their own unique expression, yet conjoined as to optimize the workspace.

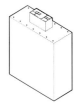

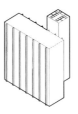
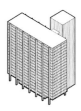

1. Modern tower
2. Columns move to the façade
3. Core is moved outside
4. Program tower and service tower

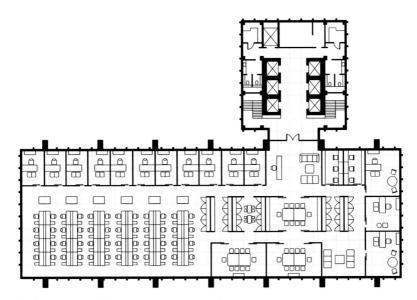

1. Modern tower, 2. Columns move to the façade,
3. Core is moved outside,
4. Program tower and service tower
Evolution of the core separating
from the interior of the building.

SIAMESE CORE

STRUCTURALIST CORE

Louis Kahn's explorations on structuralist ideas are visible in the Richards Medical Center. The project is arranged in a modular formation of "autonomous spatial units."[14] Each module is configured by a square plan and two columns on the face of each side of the square. Between the columns, service cores could plug in as needed, differentiating service spaces from serviced ones. The plan could expand in any direction as the system allowed for an additive process for expansion or contraction. The cores, in this case, do not serve any structural function. They are service attachments to the modular system.

14 Hertzberger, Herman, and John Kirkpatrick. *Architecture and Structuralism: The Ordering of Space*. Nai010 Publishers, 2015.

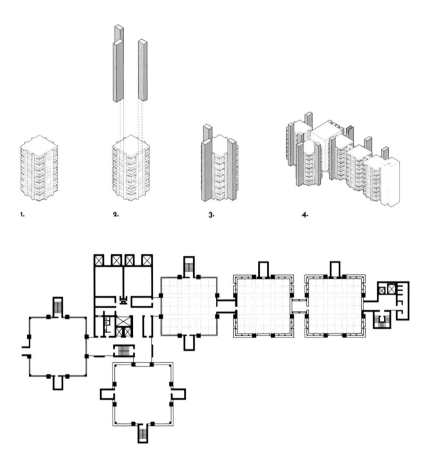

Richards Medical Research Laboratories,
Louis Kahn,
Philadelphia, USA. 1965
Diagram of core being used not as a structural
element but as a plugin service element.

STRUCTURALIST CORE

METABOLIC CORE

The postwar era during the second half of the twentieth century in Japan began a reconstruction period that would allow Japanese architects to reclaim a role in city making. For Tange, architecture should have the capacity to develop and grow organically depending on the needs of the city. At the level of architecture, this meant that buildings could be reduced to a core element which would hold plug-in components. For the Shizuoka Press and Broadcasting Center, office capsules would attach to a service core. The capsules could be added organically, allowing the building to grow with time reflecting the demand of the market.

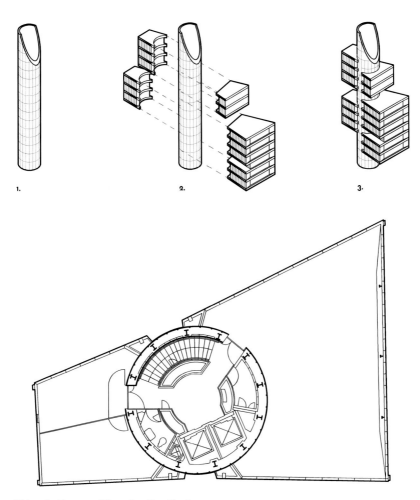

Shizuoka Press and Broadcasting Center,
Kenzo Tange,
Tokyo, Japan. 1967
Axon of plug-in units attaching to the core
and plan of core services.

METABOLIC CORE

INFRASTRUCTURAL CORE

A few years after Tange's tower, Kurokawa would propose a housing capsule tower that would focus on the lifespan of buildings as the parameter for metabolic growth. The capsules are designed to be changed every 30 years while the core is designed for a 200-year lifespan.[15] This addresses the continuity of use for a building in Tokyo beyond the typical 30-year replacement of an entire building. The core, in this sense, has an element of long-lasting permanence that becomes an infrastructural component of the city.

15 Koolhaas, Rem, et al. *Project Japan: Metabolism Talks* ... Taschen, 2011.

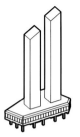
1.
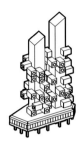
2.
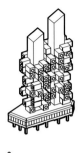
3.
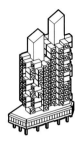
4.

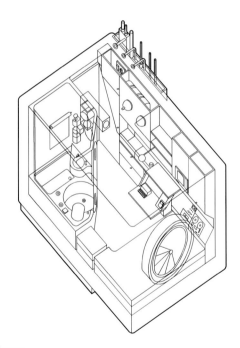

Nakagin Capsule Tower,
Kisho Kurokawa,
Tokyo, Japan. 1972
Diagram of unit aggregation over time.

INFRASTRUCTURAL CORE

TENTACLE CORE

At first glance, the proposal for the Perm museum by Valerio Olgiati seems to stack boxes of different proportions one on top of the other. The façade seems to be performing a structural and ornamental role with a structural pattern. Upon further analysis, the different boxes are held by an inner truss that spans from the core, similar to two arms stretching horizontally from the body to support some weight. These arms are arranged in cruciform formation and vary in length depending on the size of box they will hold. The core then acts more like a body with multiple arms spanning in all four perpendicular directions.

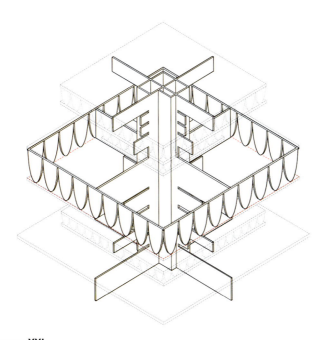

Perm Museum XXI,
Valerio Olgiati,
Perm, Russia. 2008

TENTACLE CORE

FAÇADE CORE

Similar to the 1958 Inland Steel Building by SOM, the Kitchen tower uses the core as an architectural service element separate from the programmed space. In this case, the core does not bundle all the services but it distributes them as smaller cores around the tower, serving as the primary structure for the tower as well as its tectonic expression. Each smaller core-column can be designed independently or have a unique expression in order to serve as the ornamental façade of the building.

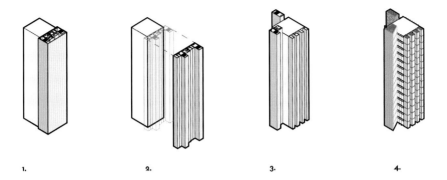

1. 2. 3. 4.

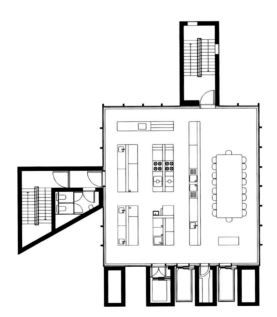

Kitchen Tower XDGA
Anderlecht,
Belgium. 2011
The decentralization of the core allows for
the core to be used as the expression of the
façade.

FAÇADE CORE

OBESE CORE

The City History Museum in Antwerp invites the public into the building through a continuous open space coming from the plaza and ending on the rooftop. This continuous spiral promenade around the massing is achieved by stacking and rotating gallery boxes that are held up by trusses spanning from the core. This allows the galleries to form the spiraling void with no column support. To further enhance this condition of a void carving the mass with no columns, undulating glass panels follow the path without any mullions or additional structural support.

261

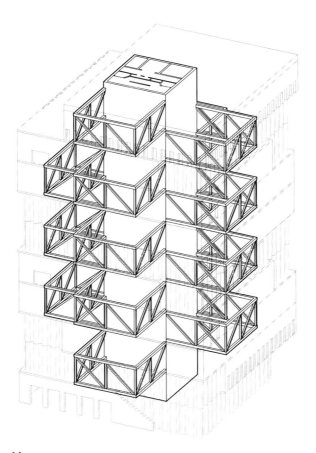

City History Museum
MAS,
Neutelings Riedijk Architects,
Antwerp, Belgium. 2010

OBESE CORE

MODULAR STACKING

Developed for the Montreal World Expo in 1967, Habitat 67 showcased a new method of construction for the time through prefabrication that would allow for a self-supporting stacking of identical concrete modules. The amorphous pattern generated by the stacking was aimed at showing the variety of spaces that could be created from a singular module; 158 apartments were originally achieved, each displaying a variability in size based on the arrangement and amount of modules used.

263

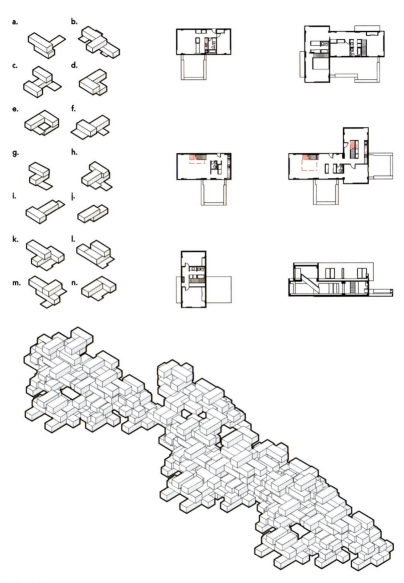

Habitat 67,
Moshe Safdie,
Montreal, Canada. 1967
The aggregation of prefabricated
modular units allows for a
formless composition.

MODULAR STACKING

MODULAR SYSTEM

Neumann's additive process to architecture follows an anti-modernist approach to building space. His strategies antecede that of European structuralism and would lay the foundation for such theories. Through this building as well as his previous studies, Neumann engaged the repetition of a module to produce a variety of space in an additive process. The module serves as space and structure and provides the logic for a three-dimensional patterning that informs the language for entrances, fenestrations, and so on.

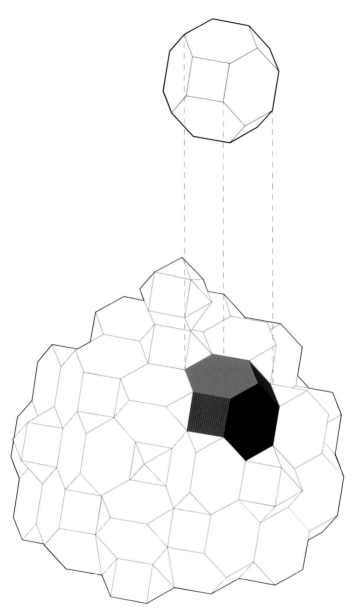

Synagogue,
Alfred Neumann and Zvi Hecker,
Negev Desert,
Israel. 1967–1969

MODULAR SYSTEM

PREFAB STACKING

Seven prefabricated pieces are stacked in a helix configuration achieving a structural equilibrium. The idea of prefabrication is to use ready-made structural pieces that can be carefully reconfigured to produce a virtual demarcation of an area. The house itself could be said to be formless as the stacking of linear pieces pierces the boundaries of a virtual platonic box form. Form is elusive as the system re-enforces an open space.

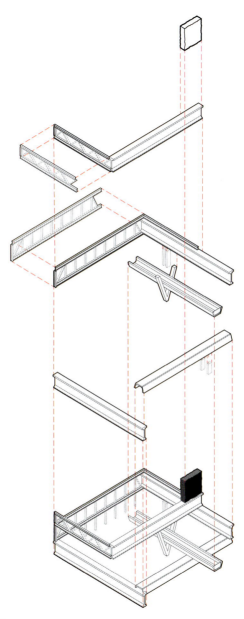

Hemeroscopium House,
Ensamble Studio,
Madrid, Spain. 2008

PREFAB STACKING

I-BEAM STACKING

Following the traditional log cabin construction, I-beams are stacked in a checkered pattern to form a three-story house. The stacked beams at the periphery allow for a structure-free space in the middle, while the stacks themselves become façade elements that directly reveal the structural system. The pattern formed by the solid beams and gaps between the beams form the fenestration logic.

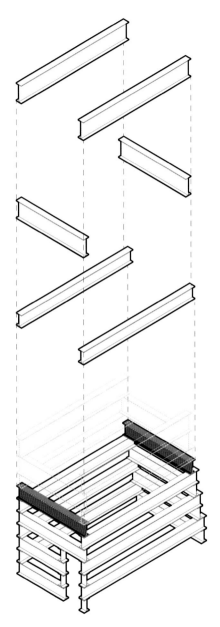

Log H,
Mount Fuji Architects Studio,
Tokyo, Japan. 2014

I-BEAM STACKING

PREFORM STACKING

Sectional extrusions of house sections create bars that stack and intersect one with the other. The shape of the section is a metaphoric gesture of a "haus" as well as a structural configuration for a self-standing structure. The stacking bars produce an "affect," as described by Eisenman, of Weak Form.[16] The agglomeration of bars is meant to be read as a spatial system rather than a strong formal gesture; instead, form is also part of the system as well as an element.

Michael Meredith and Hilary Sample investigate this system through a series of software designs like "JAM" where an algorithm simulates the piling of sticks. Scale is non-important for the system as it can be adapted.

16 Corbo, Stefano. *From Formalism to Weak Form: The Architecture and Philosophy of Peter Eisenman*. Routledge, 2020.

271

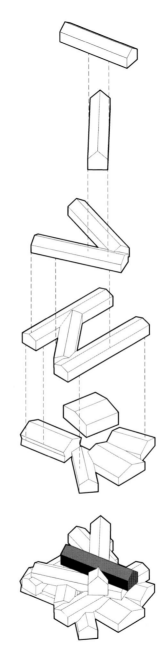

Vitrahaus,
Herzog and de Meuron,
Weil am Rhein,
Germany. 2009

PREFORM STACKING

INTERLOCKING

For the New Deichman Main Library 2009 competition in Oslo, Norway, Toyo Ito proposed an entire building composed of variations of three geometries that interlock like crystals. The polyhedron formations produced an autonomous spatial system that could expand or contract depending on the program needed. Although that competition was not won, the system was tested again for the Toyo Ito Museum of Architecture in Imabari. Much smaller in scale than the library competition, this museum explores interlocking geometries using Octahedrons, Tetrahedrons, and Cuboctahedrons with prefabricated steel plates as structure and finish. The tilted planes of the polyhedrons accentuate the volumetric space.

273

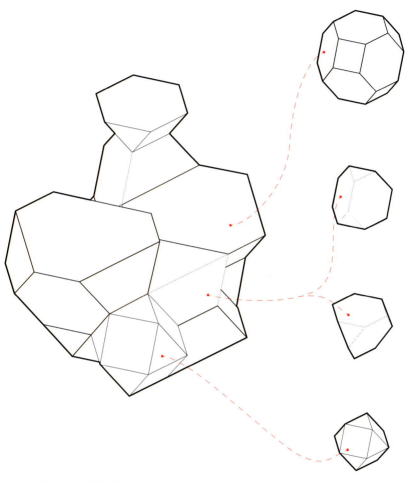

Toyo Ito Museum of Architecture,
Toyo Ito,
Imabari, Japan. 2011

INTERLOCKING

GROUND STACKING

Thirty-one housing bar blocks are stacked around open courtyards in order to create a vertical village that disrupts the typical housing typologies of Singapore. As the name of the project shows, these housing bar blocks are crossed intricately and form a three-dimensional interlace. Each block rooftop serves as a ground for the top block. This makes the condition of figure-ground obsolete as the massings serve as both figure and ground for the mass above.

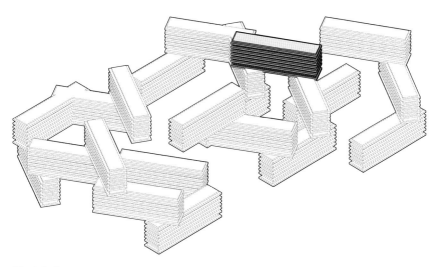

The Interlace,
OMA,
Singapore. 2013

GROUND STACKING

COURSING

Composed of an oversized stacking of concrete blocks, the building achieves a formal composition out of the system itself. The checker pattern stacking allows for an overall reading of the building with its openings in direct correlation to the gaps between modules. There are no fenestrations in the traditional sense of window element; instead, the reading of solid and void indicate where openings should occur.

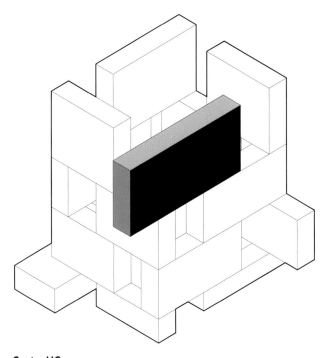

Innovation Center UC,
Alejandro Aravena,
Santiago, Chile. 2014

COURSING

FOUND SYSTEM

Inside the main hall of the Chicago Cultural Center, a series of slender pedestals held an array of tiny objects during the 2015 Chicago Architecture Biennale. These were compositions of found household objects that when populated with scaled human figures would form spatial systems. What at first glance may seem like a stack of potato chips or staples reveals a diagram for contemporary spatial configurations where the elements form the structure, ornament, and spatial logic.

279

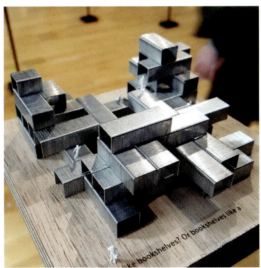

Architecture Is Everywhere,
Sou Fujimoto,
Chicago, USA. 2015
Photos taken from the Chicago
Architecture Biennial 2015.

FOUND SYSTEM

TO/T
AS   ME
DOLOO

Y
THO—
Y

Concluding Analysis and Speculations

New methods of fabrication have been exploring the merger between elements and systems as fluid spaces. This condition is more apparent in parallel industries like furniture design, boat design, car design, and aeronautical design, which integrate structure, form, space, and finish. In the works of Joris Laarman Lab, pieces of furniture can be understood as a holistic system, which, when scaled up, can become a new spatial logic. In the Maker Chairs series, three chairs follow the same form but are constructed through different systems. Reverse engineering of the process of design reveals, first, a form is produced based on certain desired parameters (ex ergonomics). Second, once the form is produced, then the designer must investigate which system is suitable for building the form in a way that the system of construction is structural as well as ornamental in order to create an aesthetic effect.

Maker Chairs,
Joris Laarman, 2014

The series presents multiple chairs, all following the exact same form composed from a single surface manipulation. When comparing three of them, one chair is made of hexagonal wooden pieces that have been CNC and glued in place, one chair is made from wooden puzzle pieces, and one chair is made of a metal mesh. Form alone does not differentiate their design. They rely on their distinct fabrication techniques to produce significantly different effects. Someone might find the metal mesh chair to be colder, and less comfortable, for example, regardless of the fact that it follows the same ergonomics as the wooden ones. While the form has a certain function, it relies on its elements and system of fabrication to achieve the full effect of warmth and comfort. The Maker Chair series reveals a compositional progression that can be analogous to a methodology for contemporary architecture. Form is autonomous and virtual, manipulated for contextualization (legal or phenomenological) or semiotic. Once a desired virtual form is achieved, elements are diffused as a system of fabrication. One system must align with the desired effect while at the same time forming a spatial logic. The system must also adapt its density in order to accommodate structural requirements at certain points, produce opacities and transparencies, avoiding unnecessary ornaments.

Toyo Ito's Serpentine Pavilion project from 2002 can serve as an architectural example for this process. Sitting in London's Kensington Gardens, this platonic cube form anchors the site as a clear contrast between nature and pure form. As a hexahedron, there is no distinction between sidewalls or roof as these do not exist in the composition, and they are all to be treated as equal faces of the form. A steel frame structure follows an indiscriminate geometrical, almost random, pattern on all faces of the form. Despite the effect of randomness, the pattern makes a clear structural system not only for tension forces of the top face but also for compression forces on the side faces. The pattern is then infilled with metal plates following a checker pattern. This grants the system lateral stability, as well as a system for voids that serve as fenestrations. There are no windows, or doors in the traditional sense, only a solid and void structural, three-dimensional pattern. This integrated approach to form, system, and elements provides the solution for structure, effect, ornament, and space.

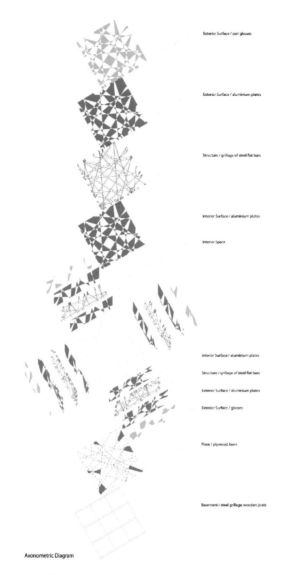

Axonometric Diagram

**Serpentine Gallery Pavilion,
Toyo Ito,
London, UK. 2002**

    Platonic forms are used again by Ito to further explore three-dimensional structural patterns for the new Deichman Main Library competition in Oslo, Norway, in 2009. Using an Octahedron, Tetrahedron, and Cuboctahedron, a rectangular prism is composed out of the stacking of these formal structural elements. Here, elements are equal to the structure. While the competition was not won, a prototype of the system was built in Imabari in 2011 as the Toyo Ito Museum of Architecture where this spatial system is tested.

Perhaps the most iconic of these explorations was initiated with the Forum for Dance, Music, and Visual Culture competition in Ghent, Belgium, in 2004. Adjusted to infill an odd curvilinear site within the old City of Ghent, an almost oval form is placed to house a concert hall with 1,800 seats. Despite having a defined program, the form is treated with a three-dimensional single surface pattern of caves. While the entry was not accepted, the concept was carried out for the National Taichung Theater (2016). Having a larger site to operate with, the building is formed as a large rectangular prism and contextualized through its placement on the site. The form sits back to provide a large entry plaza that aligns with a green urban axis. With a capacity of 2,014 seats, the system is adapted into six stories and larger performance space. Regardless of the change of program requirements, the system is autonomous and can be deformed, adapted, and manipulated to achieve different scales within the same form, while merging walls, columns, floors, ceilings as one single continuous surface.

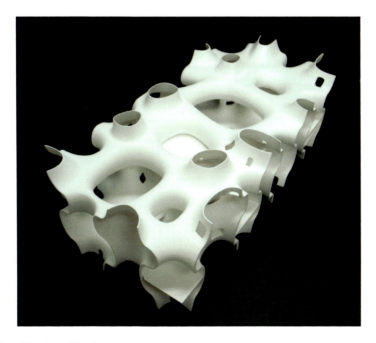

National Taichung Theater,
Toyo Ito,
Taichung, Taiwan. 2016

These two variations of Ito's holistic projects reveal the possibility for a methodology where the form is defined first, followed by an integral system, or having the system first, and producing a form directly from it. The end result should have the same aim, integrating form, system, and elements. While the same form may be achieved through different systems, or systems are more susceptible to certain forms, the architect's role is to understand the spatial qualities that can be achieved from the deformation of topologies and the selection of systems that can produce a form effectively.

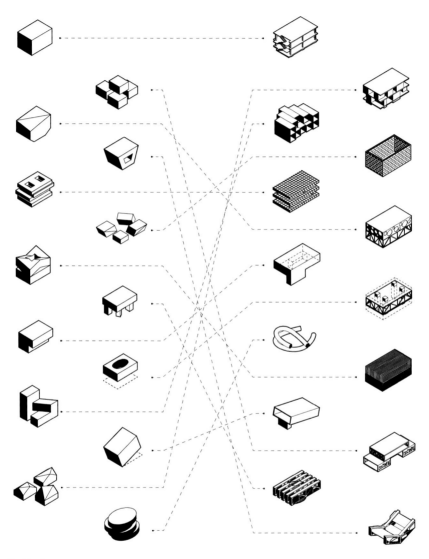

To/Ty diagram
Diagram of different topologies being built through different typological systems.

SIX EXPERIMENTS

As a theoretical proposition, topology and typology were tested out through six hypothetical projects ranging in scale and location. The aim was to investigate the contextualization of topology, spatial systems for making form, and the relation between program, form, and system.

1.

Louisville Children's Museum

2.

Helsinki Public Library

3.

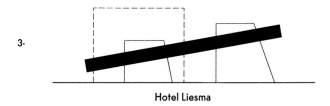

Hotel Liesma

Elevations as figureground diagrams.

4.

Dubai Expo Korean Pavilion

5.

Main Library of Gwangju

6.

Space Salim

Figure 1 Louisville Children's Museum.
Figure 2 Helsinki Public Library.
Figure 3 Hotel Liesma.
Figure 4 Dubai Expo Korean Pavilion. Figure 5 Main Library of Gwangju. Figure 6 Space Salim

SIX EXPERIMENTS

SIX EXPERIMENTS

1.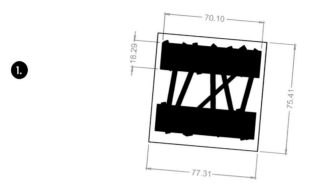

2.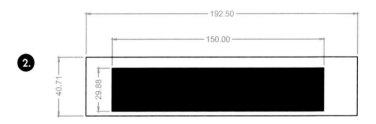

3.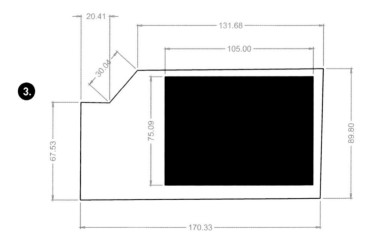

Figureground plans.
1. Louisville Children's Museum
2. Helsinki Public Library
3. Hotel Liesma
4. Dubai Expo Korean Pavilion
5. Main Libary of Gwangju
6. Space Salim

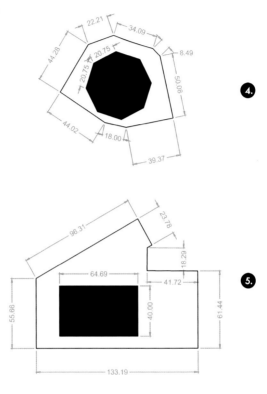

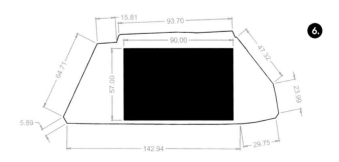

SIX EXPERIMENTS

THREE-DIMENSIONAL STRUCTURAL PATTERN – DUBAI PAVILION

As a formal abstraction of a traditional Korean octagonal gift box, this proposal for the Dubai Expo Korean pavilion assembles a three-dimensional patterning through the stacking of diagonal sections. As each section stacks on the previous one, it rotates by 45 degrees to produce a coursing checkered pattern. Each section is structural onto itself, not requiring any additional elements but the pure formal system. This simple spatial configuration adheres to the narrative required by the competition brief, to address the contemporary notion of mobility. Moving from the Cartesian axis to the topological understanding of space, one should move in all directions and utilize every surface regardless of orientation, especially when society has also evolved in instant mobility of information through digitization. Through the repetition of the sectional module and its reorientation through stacking, the same space is seen as inverted, rotated, or inflected allowing for different perceptions of the same space and their different potential uses. Surfaces that are inverted are used for projections, tilted surfaces are used for sitting, and lecturing, while flat surfaces are used for collective gatherings. As Korea leads the world in information technology, this gift box intends to be a present for the future of spatial relations where architecture is an autonomous scaffolding of information. This project intends to demonstrate how architecture needs to adapt and integrate into the new era of augmented and virtual realities serving as a backdrop setting. This means that as a scaffolding, it needs to optimize its form, system, and elements through their integration, avoiding unnecessary ornamentation.

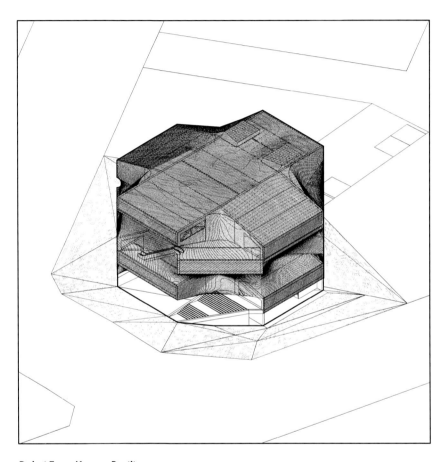

Dubai Expo Korean Pavilion,
PRAUD,
Dubai, UAE. 2018

THREE-DIMENSIONAL SRUCTURAL PATTERN – DUBAI PAVILION

TOPOLOGY

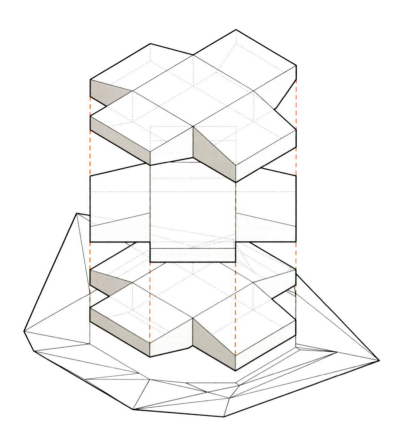

1. Traditional Korean Gift Box
2. Abstracted Topology
3. Massing as System
4. Deformations
5. Re-wrapping

1.   2.   3.   4.   5.

295

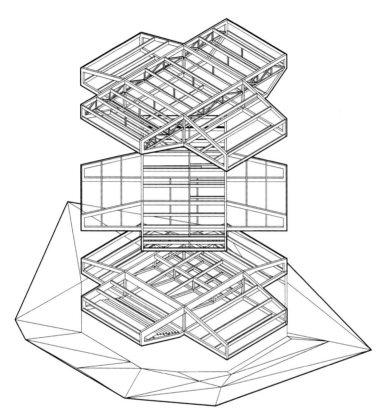

Structural Frames:
Consulted by LERA, structural cross frames stack on top of each other autonomously, forming large catelevers, and spatial diversity through the simple 45 degree rotation of each cross.

TOPOLOGY

STRUCTURAL GROUND – GWANGJU LIBRARY

The transformative relationship between ground and form has been explored through the dissociation of the figure-ground reading of a building. Ground can be explored as an extension in a single surface project or its sectioning in order to accommodate a program in it. Ground can also be explored as a continuous spatial system; grounds can stack if they follow structural forms. The Gwangju Library explores a multiple ground system where sections meet to form large collective fluid spaces. As a balancing act, a ground above joins a ground below at four points on the perimeter of the maximum volume. A mirroring effect occurs where the visitor would experience the fluid space below their feet as well as above their head recognizing the space where one walks is also the ceiling for the space below.

The project intends to demonstrate the future library as a public ground where knowledge is collected and disseminated through human interaction and their relationship to their context. The ground manipulation seeks to frame specific views to the surrounding farmlands in the northwest, park system in the southwest, urban fabric to the southeast, remaining factory to the northeast, and the sky at the top center. This framing of surrounding environments through the manipulation of the ground allows for the distinction of space while maintaining the same spatial logic and space patterning.

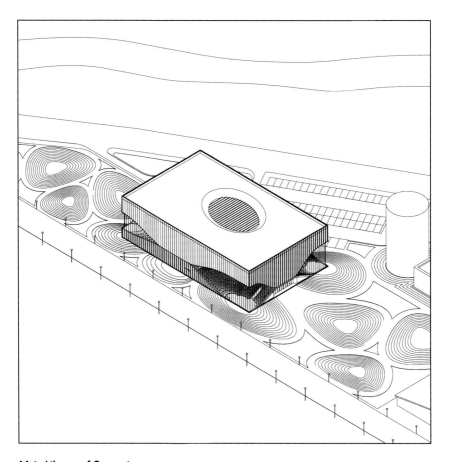

Main Library of Gwangju,
PRAUD,
Gwangju, Korea. 2020

STRUCTURAL GROUND – GWANGJU LIBRARY

TOPOLOGY

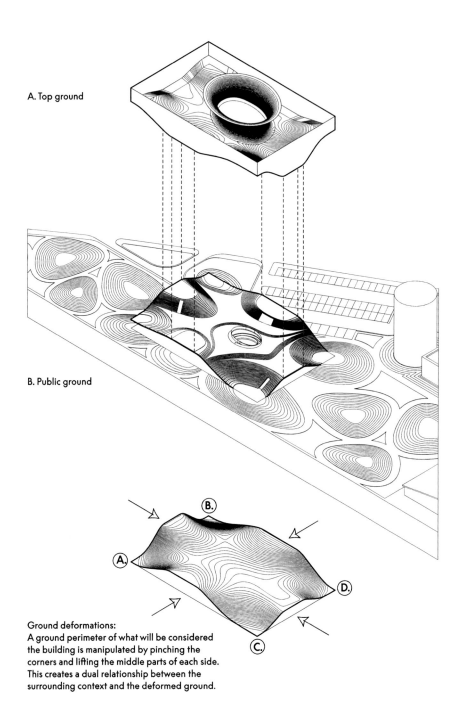

A. Top ground

B. Public ground

Ground deformations:
A ground perimeter of what will be considered the building is manipulated by pinching the corners and lifting the middle parts of each side. This creates a dual relationship between the surrounding context and the deformed ground.

A. Structural Concept

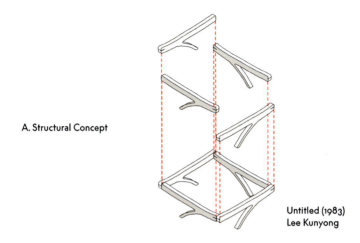

Untitled (1983)
Lee Kunyong

B. Cores as connection points between grounds

C. Balancing grounds

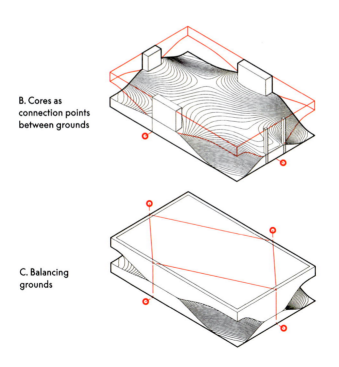

TOPOLOGY

FIGURE OVER GROUND

The main concept of this project is to elevate the massing for a new hotel above the ground level. There are two major purposes to this approach: to have a widely open covered public park on the ground level for public functions and to provide a better view to the Baltic Sea from each hotel room over a thick canopy of trees that would block the views otherwise.

Every single room has a direct view toward the sea by tilting the volume at a slight angle. This new mat-type building is held by large coned megacolumns. The multiple structural cones contain public programs such as a music cafe, restaurants, a conference hall, and a swimming pool. By having private hotel rooms separated from the ground level, the whole ground level acts as a public music park filled with dynamic and cultural venues that merge hotel guests and tourists who visit the city.

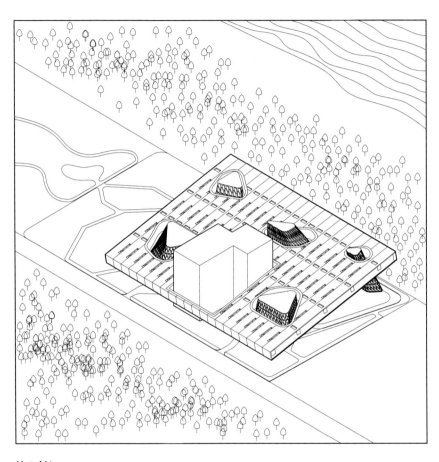

Hotel Liesma,
PRAUD,
Jurmala, Latvia. 2011

FIGURE OVER GROUND

FIGURE OVER GROUND

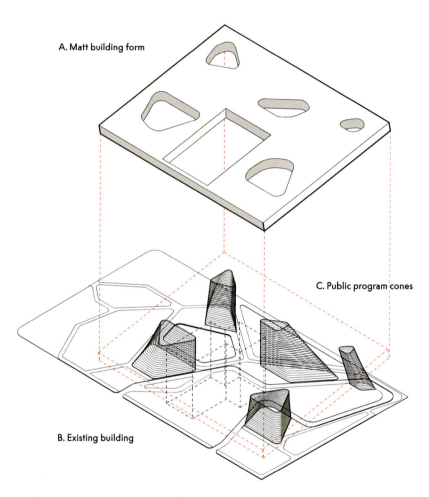

A. Matt building form

B. Existing building

C. Public program cones

In order to produce a covered plaza that will allow for public events, such as concerts and music festivals, a horizontal mass is levitated above the grounds.

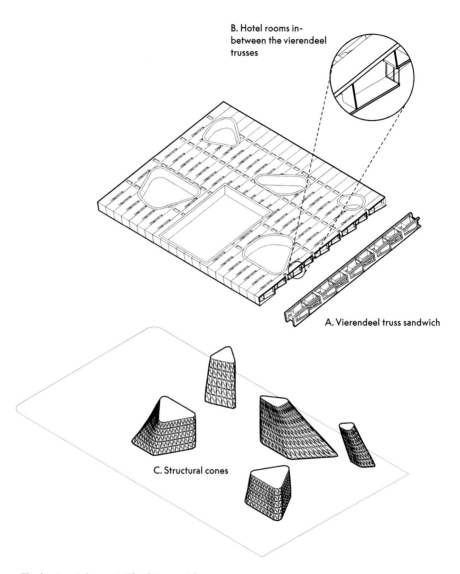

B. Hotel rooms in-between the vierendeel trusses

A. Vierendeel truss sandwich

C. Structural cones

The horizontal mass is tilted to provide views to the Balcan Sea over the canopy of trees. The series of hotel rooms are stepped between vierendeel trusses.

FIGURE OVER GROUND

FRENCH FRIES SANDWICH

In order to attract more people to the downtown area of Louisville, the Children's Museum is conceptualized as a series of Urban Spaces that creates a "Cultural Campus." These open spaces are created by the massing of each site, in order to enforce a continuous link between the hi-tech start-up incubator, Public Library, and Children's Museum. The museum program mass is split into two buildings, creating an open public space in between. This new urban space becomes an anchor point that gravitates public access from the library on the south and from the park on the south-east side. A series of circulation bridges not only structures potential exhibition spaces in the museum, but creates visual and spatial interactions between the museum program and open public space. Six bridges loosely define the public space in the middle so that the space can provide a unique atmosphere different from the park on the south-east side. Yellow boxes in between black-horizontal bars function as structural elements as well as black box programmatic elements. These boxes have interactive façades that will indicate exhibition programs so that people from outside can also see what is happening inside of the museum. This significant massing strategy allows for an interaction to occur between people working in the building as well as visitors to the museum, creating a cultural mixing for all ages.

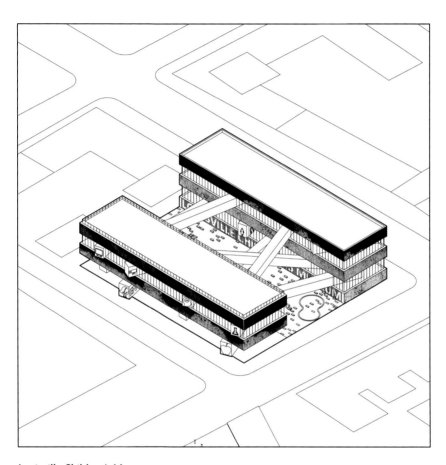

Louisville Children's Museum,
PRAUD,
Louisville, USA. 2014

FRENCH FRIES SANDWICH

FRENCH FRIES SANDWICH

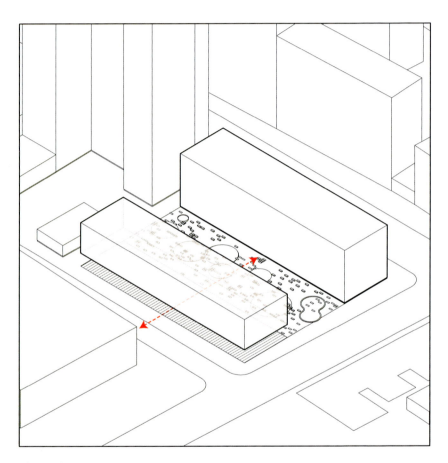

Massing Intent
To produce a series of open space connections with the surrounding context, a bar is placed on the street side to form the block's edge, while another bar is levitated in front of the library in order to create a portal for a courtyard space.

System concept:
"French Fries Sandwich"

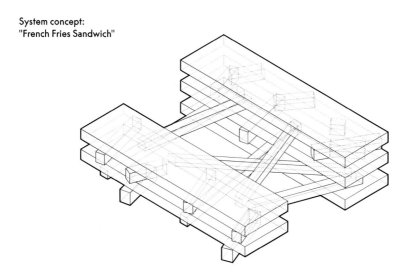

1. Object Column and slab:
With the on the south and from the
park on the south-east side

2. Object slab:
With the on the south and from
the park on the south-east side

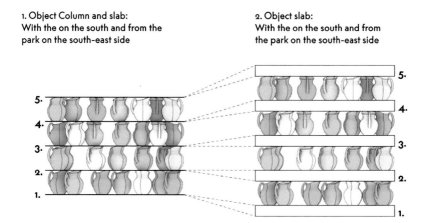

Refer to image on page 241.

FRENCH FRIES SANDWICH

HORIZONTAL THIRD SPACE

This building investigates the possibility of inviting the public by exposing its programs as part of a public space. Instead of hiding programs from the public eye by putting them inside the building, the building splits vertically to create an open plaza in between a podium and a floating mass where the most public program can happen as a marketplace. This covered marketplace resembles the spirit of an old market in Seoul, where various activities can happen under one roof allowing for the possibility of diversity.

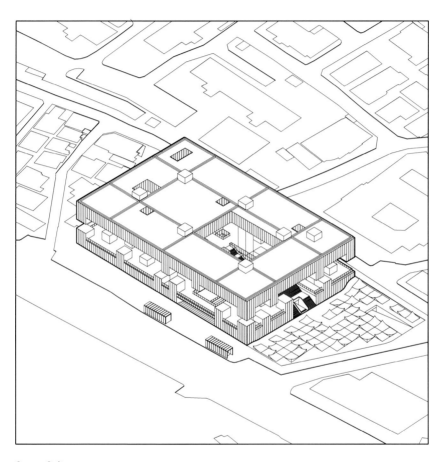

Space Salim,
PRAUD,
Seoul, Korea. 2016

HORIZONTAL THIRD SPACE

HORIZONTAL THIRD SPACE

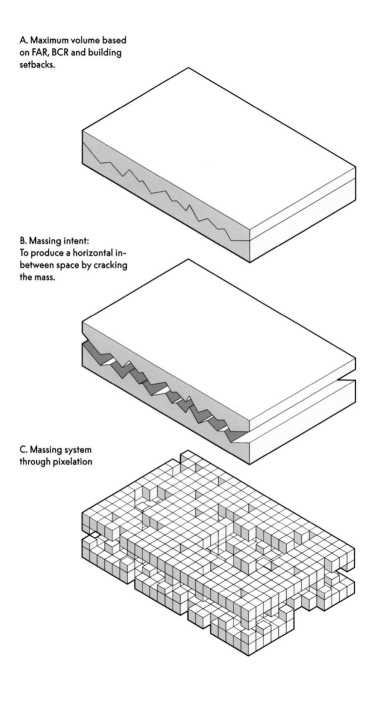

A. Maximum volume based on FAR, BCR and building setbacks.

B. Massing intent: To produce a horizontal in-between space by cracking the mass.

C. Massing system through pixelation

311

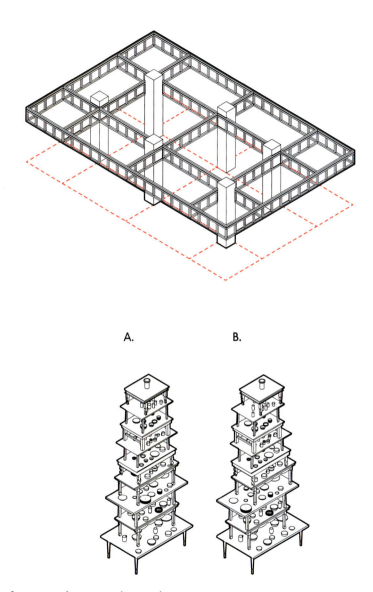

A. B.

A configuration of trusses and core columns produce a table structure able to hold independent components.

HORIZONTAL THIRD SPACE

VERTICAL THIRD SPACE

When we think of the title for this competition, "The Heart of the Metropolis," it makes us analyze the civic duty and responsibility that a future library will have for the city of Helsinki. The intent of this project is to propose a building that serves a larger civic function by creating a public space for congregation at an urban scale, not only as an interior logic (library as a living room) but directly as a massing strategy that allows for public appropriation (building as a living room).

Because the building is oriented north to south, a vertical doughnut is stretched along the north and south axis to create a large elevated atrium that serves as the city's public living room, a free space donated back to the city. This strategy allows for the library collection to be elevated as a beacon of education while all other programming is organized around the atrium.

In order to create flexibility between the public educational program and the social living room, larger elements are encapsulated into structural tubes that sit within two mega-trusses. This allows for a duality of spatial relation where programs, like the cinema, can be inside one of the tubes while lounges connect to the atrium.

The main goal for this building will be to provide the sense of social interaction and mixing, views to the city, connections to the neighboring cultural facilities, while encompassing a new vision for education in a single building.

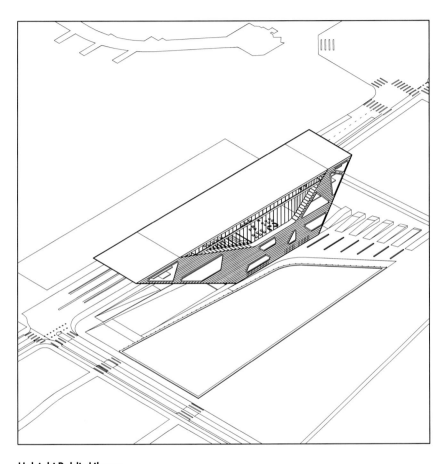

Helsinki Public Library,
PRAUD,
Helsinki, Finland. 2012

VERTICAL THIRD SPACE

TOPOLOGY

The required massing for the library could fit as a single bar spread across the width of the site. This would block the buildings north of the site. By lifting up the sides of the bar, the back buildings gain some views, the library opens up to the park on the west, meets the height of the surrounding buildings on the east, and creates an elevated urban living room with views of the city and its landmarks.

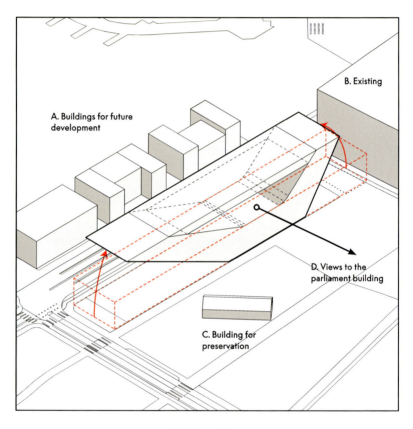

A. Buildings for future development
B. Existing
C. Building for preservation
D. Views to the parliament building

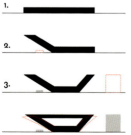

1. Maximum volume
2. Open mass to the park on the west.
3. Match height with neighbohring buildings.
4. Connect with a top bar to create a covered public space.

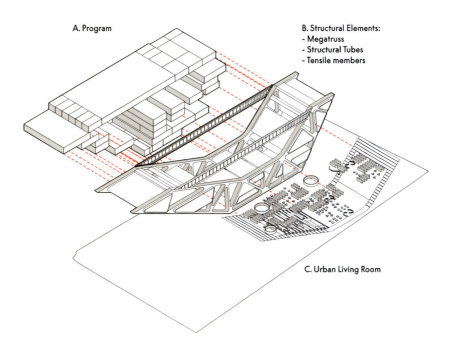

System Logic

1. 2. 3. 4.

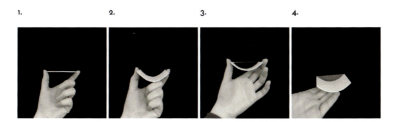

TOPOLOGY

FOUR HOUSES

On the practical side, the methodology was tested through four real projects of similar scale and program. Due to the local construction techniques and codes, four different construction systems were explored through concrete, steel, wood framing, and concrete blocks. The massing intents relate to the opportunities and limitations of their respective systems.

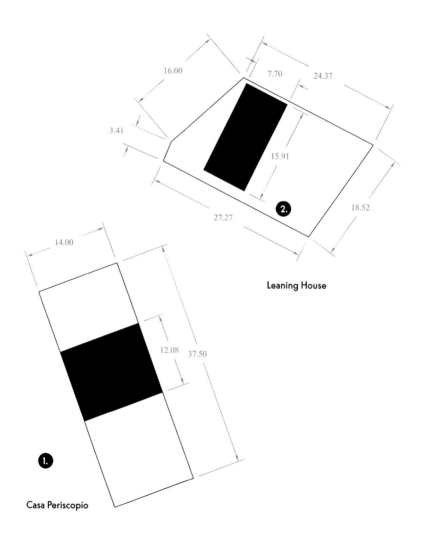

Leaning House

1. Casa Periscopio

317

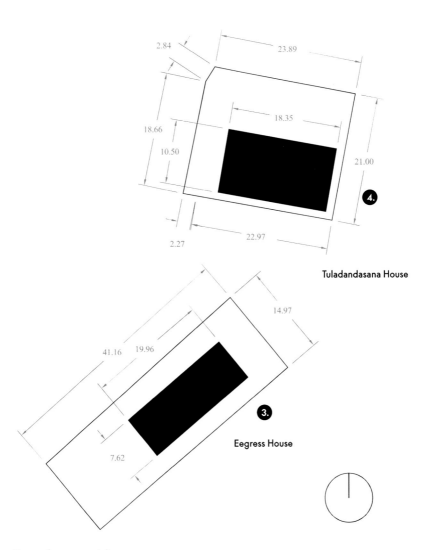

Tuladandasana House

Eegress House

Plans as figureground diagrams.

FOUR HOUSES

FOUR HOUSES

Casa Periscopio
Single Family
Area:
Costa del Sol, El Salvador (2012)

Leaning House
Single Family
Area:
Cheongpyeong, South Korea (2014)

EEgress House
Three Family Building
Area:
Boston, MA (2018)

4.
Tuladandasana House
Two Family House
Area:
Pohang, South Korea (2018)

FOUR HOUSES

MASSING - INTENT

Figure 1
Tip-Toe
In order to obtain better views of the ocean over the surrounding trees and neighboring houses, the massing is pushed vertically.

Figure 2
Anti-gravity lean
Surrounded by mountains, this massing opens up to the south sun and views mimicking the mountain range angles by tilting on an edge.

Figure 3
Tetris
This multi-family looks to maintain the presence of an absolute form through an interlocking of its pieces, although it has let a piece go.

Figure 4
Warrior III
In order to build this house over an existing house, the massing intent is to balance a new structure with minimum amount of legs over the existing structure, almost like a warrior III (tuladandasana) yoga pose balancing act.

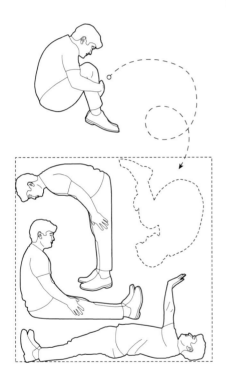

MASSING - INTENT

MASSING - STRATEGY

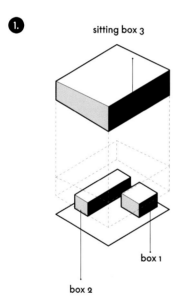 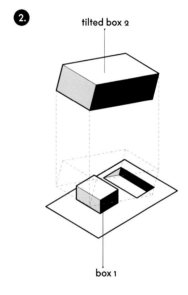

Figure 1
Stacking
To achieve the intention of looking over the neighbours, the house is separated into three distinct volumes. Two smaller volumes for the structure that holds an upper volume.

Figure 2
Tilting
As a way to integrate the landscape to the interior space while creating a fluid interior, the house is tilted like a box.

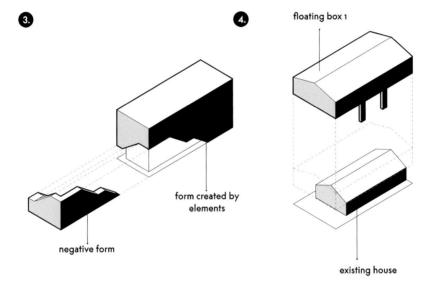

Figure 3
Breaking
As the stairs form the massing expression, the negative space is removed, revealing the stair geometry.

Figure 4
Mounting
To avoid disturbing the lower house, an independent upper home is mounted on top by means of a steel structural table that gently straddles the lower house.

MASSING - STRATEGY

SYSTEM

Figure 1
CMU
This is a vertical aggregate system. This is used to create stacking volumes

Figure 2
Concrete
The ability to span horizontally, allows for a concrete frame to be tilted while reinforcing the volumetric reading.

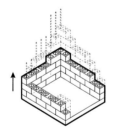
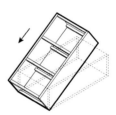

Figure 3
Wood Framing
This is a horizontal modular system that limits the openness of the volume and horizontal span.

Figure 4
Steel
Steel allows for a separation of structural frames that gives the chance to expand vertically as well as horizontally.

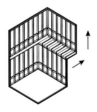

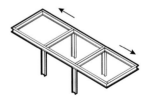

SYSTEM

PRODUCTION OF THIRD SPACE

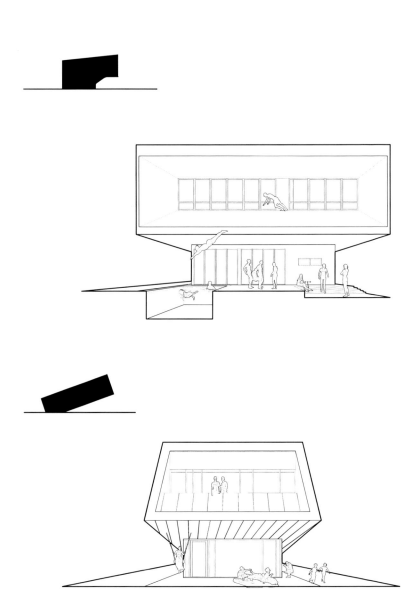

327

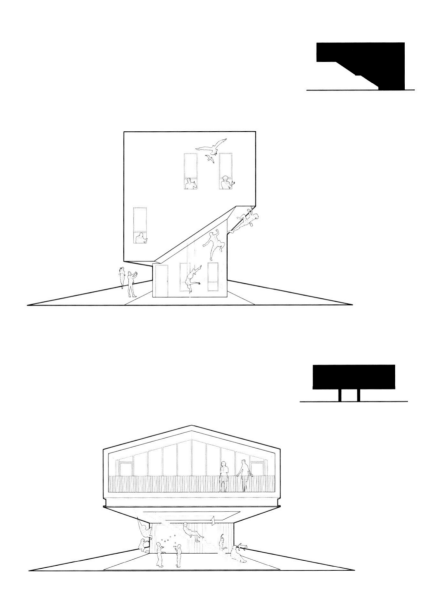

Perspectives of the third space in each house.

PRODUCTION OF THIRD SPACE

"Beyond Modernism"

In conversation with Toyo Ito
May 2020 (Seoul/Tokyo)

PRAUD   Your work has extended now over a period of five decades starting in the 1970s under the ethos of "Beyond Modernism." The 1970s is an interesting starting point as it is marked by a technocratic period coming from the 1960s High-Modernism, the space race, and the cold war.
Would you consider the decade of the 1970s in your work as an exploratory period to position the project of "Beyond Modernism"?

TI   1970年代はまだModernism Architectureを意識しており、その先の「Beyond Modernism」を考えることはしていませんでした。
I was still thinking about architecture within the framework of Modernist Architecture in the 1970s, thus I did not have the idea of "Beyond Modernism" yet at the time.

PRAUD   When I see your projects from that decade compared to the twenty-first century projects, there are several investigatory paths: White U (1976) is a formal exercise of inhabiting a predetermined form; Hotel D (1977) I read Venturi's postmodern tendencies; PMT Building in Nagoya (1978) I can read Maki's influence; and House in Kogani (1979) I could compare to Rogers's Wimbledon House for highlighting the steel frame as a technocratic approach to architecture.

TI   「「中野本町の家」は「form」をつくるという意図はなく、U字や雁行する屋根など様々な要素を用いて「空間」をつくろうとしていました。
「中野本町の家」で試みた雁行する天井、小さなカーブのような小さなエレメントをモルフェームと名付けましたが、内部空間でそれらの組み合わせをつくることに関心がありました。「Hotel D」もその試みのひとつで、ポストモダニズムの意図はありません。

328

「PMTビル名古屋」は外観のファサードは「仮面」を表現しており、内部はコルビュジエのエレメントを意図的に使用しました。そのため槇文彦氏の影響は全くありません。
「小金井の家」は鉄骨の柱と梁を用いていますが、クライアントである一般の方にプランを考えてもらうことを意識しており、取り組んでいた「商品化住宅」が建築となったもので、リチャード・ロジャース氏の影響はありません。

For the White U, the intention was not to create "form." Instead, I tried to create "space" with several elements such as the U shape and the inclining roof. I have named these small elements such as inclining ceilings and tiny curves "Morpheme," and I was mostly interested in creating an interior space by combining different Morphemes. Hotel D was also an attempt to use Morphemes and there was no intention for postmodernism. The façade of the PMT Building – Nagoya represents a "mask" and for the interior space I intentionally utilized the elements by Le Corbusier. It was not influenced by Mr. Fumihiko Maki at all. I used a steel frame for the House in Koganei, but this is for ease of construction and to develop a plan of the house for a client who is not an architect. This attempt is based on our research project "Commercialized Residences" and not related to Mr. Richard Rogers.

PRAUD   At that point, was there a sense of also battling postmodernism?

TI   上記の通り、ポストモダニズムとの闘いは意識していませんでした。
As stated in the answer above, there was no sense of battling postmodernism at that point.

PRAUD   There is a very clear demarcation that occurs at the turn of the century, starting with the Sendai Mediatheque (2000), where your projects express a break from modernism by referencing it directly. It is no longer about finding a "post-modern" agenda or style, but truly to reflect on the adaptabilities of the modernist system along with its elements, and how to evolve them into the contemporary context. Is this a reflection on architecture not as a style but as a language?

TI 「せんだいメディアテーク」で試みたことは、自然のイメージを抽象化して内部に表現することでした。自然のイメージの抽象化はその後の私の建築で一貫して取り組んでいますが、その最も初期段階であったと思います。

My attempt for the Sendai Mediatheque was to create an abstract image of nature and to express it inside of the space. The abstraction of nature has been one of my challenging themes after Sendai Mediatheque and this project was the very initial stage of this attempt.

PRAUD I would say your work in the twenty-first century focuses more on the language of architecture through a merger of elements and systems to produce a form. This is non-stylistic, but purely spatial, and I would categorize your investigations under façade projects, column projects, wall projects, and three-dimensional holistic pattern projects.
Your column projects could be classified under Object Columns, like the Sendai Mediatheque where the column can be spatial and programmatic, or Field Columns, like the Tama Art Library (2007).
Façade projects like Tod's in Omotesando or Mikimoto in Ginza use the façade as the building structural element as well as its ornamental aesthetics.
Wall projects like the Museum Internacional del Barroco use the wall as a spatial expressive structural system that replaces the structural column grid.
All of these (wall, column, façade) projects I would say are directly referencing the Dom-ino system. Was this the intention?

TI 私のプロジェクトでは、プエブラのプロジェクトを除き、梁や壁を使用せずに主に柱を使うことで、自由で流動的な空間をつくることを試みています。そのためドミノで考えていることとは全く異なります。

Apart from Museo Internacional del Barroco in Puebla, in most of my projects I tried to create a free and fluid space by utilizing columns and not walls or beams. Thus, this is totally different from the Dom-ino system.

PRAUD In order to understand how to move "Beyond Modernism," one must start from the quintessential modernist model and distort it by inflicting a transformation of how to operate on its elements.

Was there ever an investigation on the deformation of the slab? (single surface projects, tilted sab)

TI　床スラブとしては東京オペラシティで行われた展覧会「伊東豊雄 建築I新しいリアル」、3D曲面を描く屋根スラブとしては「瞑想の森 市営斎場」、「川口めぐりの森」で実践しています。
I tried to deform the floor slab at the exhibition "Toyo Ito: The new 'Real' in Architecture" at Tokyo Opera City Gallery and the 3D curved slab at "Meiso no Mori" Municipal Funeral Hall and "Meguri no Mori" Kawaguchi City Funeral Hall.

PRAUD　I am very intrigued by your three-dimensional holistic pattern projects, Brugge, Serpentine, Toyo Ito Museum, and the National Taichung Museum Theater. These projects are no longer about the dom-ino system reference, but about an inflection on the Euclidean grid transforming into a three-dimensional system grid. Would you agree?

TI　直交軸から成る幾何学に対して別の幾何学を用いた3次元のグリッドシステムをつくろうとしてきました。特に「台中国家歌劇院」において実践をしています。
I have been trying to create a 3-dimensional grid system with geometries other than orthogonal axes. Especially for The National Taichung Theater, the 3-dimensional grid system had been explored and realized.

PRAUD　Are these investigations on three dimensionality becoming more complex as you collaborate more with engineers that understand the new paradigm?

TI　そういうことは多々あると思います。
Yes, I think that is often the case.

PRAUD　Would you say that this could potentially be the new focus for future projects?
Lastly, I would like to conclude with the question, have we ever left modernism? If the project of "Beyond Modernism" is a self-referential model, then is it an evolution of modernism? Are the three-dimensional holistic pattern projects seen as new authenticities?

TI　何度も申し上げているように、「せんだいメディアテーク」以降、建築と自然の関係をより親密にしたいとチヤレンジをしてきました。モダニズムの建築は自然から切り離された人工環境をつくることを考えてきましたが、そこに現代建築の問題があると思っています。自然との関係を大切にしていくこと、「内なる自然」という自然の抽象化という意図で、3Dや最新の技術も活用しながら「Beyond Modernism」を目指したいと思っています。

As answered many times in the above questions, I have been trying to create a closer relationship between architecture and nature after Sendai Mediatheque. Modernist Architecture tries to create an artificial space that is detached from nature, but I can say this is the major cause to the problem of Modern Architecture. I aim to go "Beyond Modernism" by creating an abstraction of nature in form of an "Inner Nature" that cherishes the relationship with nature, and I foresee this being possible through the utilization of advanced 3D technologies.

PRAUD　Thank you for your time and consideration.
Rafael Luna
rluna@praud.info
Seoul, South Korea
May 25, 2020

333

REFERENCES PER SPREAD

p. 22
Nesbitt, Kate. *Theorizing a New Agenda for Architecture: An Anthology of Architectural Theory 1965–1995.* Princeton Architectural Press, New York, NY, 2008, p. 240.

p. 24
Quincy Quatremère de. *Dictionnaire Historique D'architecture.* Librairie D'Adrien Le Clere, 1832, p. 629.
Argan, Giulio Carlo. "On The Typology of Architecture." *Theorizing a New Agenda for Architecture: An Anthology of Architectural Theory, 1965–1995,* edited by Kate Nesbitt, Princeton Architectural Press, New York, NY, 1996, pp. 242–246.
Moneo, Rafael. "On Typology." *A Journal for Ideas and Criticism in Architecture,* vol. 18, 1978, pp. 23–45.
Colquhoun, Alan. "Typology and Design Method." *Theorizing a New Agenda for Architecture: An Anthology of Architectural Theory 1965–1995,* edited by Kate Nesbitt, Princeton Architectural Press, New York, NY, 1996, pp. 250–257.

p. 24
Rossi, Aldo. *The Architecture of the City.* MIT Press, Cambridge, MA, 2007.
Vidler, Anthony. "The Third Typology." *Theorizing a New Agenda for Architecture: An Anthology of Architectural Theory 1965–1995,* edited by Kate Nesbitt, Princeton Architectural Press, New York, NY, 1996, pp. 260–263.

p. 30
Moussavi, Farshid, and Michael Kubo. *The Function of Ornament.* Actar, 2008

p. 32
Vidler, Anthony. "The Third Typology." *Theorizing a New Agenda for Architecture: An Anthology of Architectural Theory 1965–1995,* edited by Kate Nesbitt, Princeton Architectural Press, New York, NY, 1996, pp. 260–263.

p. 34
Laugier, Marc-Antoine, et al. *An Essay on Architecture.* Hennessey & Ingalls, 2009.

p. 36
Durand, Jean-Nicolas-Louis. *Precis Des Lecons D'architecture Donnees a L'Ecole Polytechnique.* Hachette Livre – BNF, 2018.

p. 40
Moneo, Rafael. "On Typology." *A Journal for Ideas and Criticism in Architecture,* vol. 18, 1978, pp. 23–45.
Quincy Quatremère de. *Dictionnaire Historique D'architecture.* Librairie D'Adrien Le Clere, 1832.

p. 65
Look at ENSAMBLE Studio's Truffle House, an experiment on prefabricated forms. "The Truffle: Ensamble-Studio." *Ensamble,* https://www.ensamble.info/thetruffle.

p. 76
"Topology." *Wikipedia,* Wikimedia Foundation, 12 Feb. 2022, https://en.wikipedia.org/wiki/Topology.

p. 78
Lynn, Greg. *Animate Form.* Princeton Architectural Press, 1998.

p. 82
Scardifield, Kate. "Soft Topologies." *KATE SCARDIFIELD,* 2018, https://www.katescardifield.com.au/soft-topologies-text.
SOFT TOPOLOGIES, Philip, Isobel Parker. *The Wind, Apparently,* UTS Gallery, Ultimo, NSW, 2018.

p. 90
Kaufmann, Emil. *Von Ledoux Bis Le Corbusier Ursprung Und Entwicklung Der Autonomen Architektur.* Gerd Hatje, 1985.

p. 92
Blanciak François. *Siteless: 1001 Building Forms.* MIT Press, 2008.

p. 104
Munari, Bruno. *Scatola Di Architettura MC 1.* Corraini, 2003.

p. 106
Munari, Bruno. *Supplemento Al Dizionario Italiano.* Muggiani, 1963.

p. 108
Venturi, Robert, et al. *Learning from Las Vegas*. The MIT Press, 2017, pp. 87–91.

p. 112
Rowe, Colin, and Fred Koetter. *Collage City*. Birkhäuser, 2009.

p. 116
Aureli, Pier Vittorio. *The Possibility of an Absolute Architecture*. MIT Press, 2011.
Maki, Fumihiko. *Investigations in Collective Form*. School of Architecture, Washington University, 2004.
Maki, Ibid., p. 6

p. 118
Maki, Fumihiko. *Investigations in Collective Form*. School of Architecture, Washington University, 2004, p. 8.
"Het Nieuwe Instituut." *Objects*, https://zoeken.hetnieuweinstituut.nl/en/objects/detail/?q=Bakema+Tel+Aviv&page=2.

p. 122
Maki, Fumihiko. *Investigations in Collective Form*. School of Architecture, Washington University, 2004, p. 14.

p. 124
Trummer, Peter. "Peter Trummer (February 22, 2012)." *YouTube*, SCI-Arc Media Archive, 7 Sept. 2017, https://youtu.be/UCbf9P9dySY.

p. 126
Breton, Andre, et al. "Cadavre Exquis [Exquisite Corpse]." *National Galleries of Scotland*, National Galleries of Scotland, 2020, https://www.nationalgalleries.org/art-and-artists/31332/cadavre-exquis-exquisite-corpse.

p. 128
Museum of Modern Art. MoMA, https://assets.moma.org/documents/moma_press-release_326503.pdf.

p. 130
Museum of Modern Art. MoMA, https://assets.moma.org/documents/moma_press-release_326374.pdf.

p. 132
Reeser, Amanda. "'We'll Have One of Each.'" *Canadian Centre for Architecture*, CCA, https://www.cca.qc.ca/en/articles/issues/25/a-history-of-references/56241/well-have-one-of-each.
"WE'LL HAVE ONE OF EACH", Tschumi, Bernard. *The Manhattan Transcripts*. Academy Editions, 1981.

p. 134
Werlemann, Hans, et al. *Seattle Public Library*. OMA/LMN, 2001.

p. 136
"Y2K House." OMA, https://www.oma.com/projects/y2k-house.

p. 140
Rowe, Colin, and Fred Koetter. *Collage City*. Birkhäuser, 2009.

p. 144
Friedman, Yona. *Yona Friedman: Pro Domo*. ACTAR, 2006.

p. 156
"Will Alsop – Nothing Is Lost." *YouTube*, 9 Oct. 2015, https://youtu.be/OSFgWR7Qepg.

p. 165
Argan, Giulio Carlo. "On the Typology of Architecture." *Theorizing a New Agenda for Architecture: An Anthology of Architectural Theory 1965–1995*, edited by Kate Nesbitt, Princeton Architectural Press, New York, NY, 1996, pp. 242–246.

p. 176
Jeanneret, Pierre. "Five Points Towards a New Architecture." *Programs and Manifestoes on 20th-Century Architecture*, edited by Ulrich Conrads, MIT Press, Cambridge, MA, 1971, pp. 59–62.

p. 180
Johnson, Philip, and Mark Wigley. *Deconstructivist Architecture*. Little, Brown, 1988.
"DECONSTRUCTIVIST ARCHITECTURE." *https://www.moma.org/Calendar/*

Exhibitions/1813, MoMA, Mar. 1988, https://
assets.moma.org/documents/moma_
press-release_327505.pdf. Accessed 15
Feb. 2022.

p. 190
Mortice, Zach, et al. "Fazlur Khan
Converged Engineering, Architecture at
the Top of the World." *Redshift EN*, 11 Nov.
2020, https://redshift.autodesk.com/
fazlur-khan/.

p. 198
"O-14." *Reiser+Umemoto, RUR Architecture
DPC*, https://www.reiser-umemoto.com/
selected-projects/o-14.

p. 200
Pedreschi, R, Theodossopoulos, D, *ICE
Proceedings, Structures and Buildings*, Vol
160, Issue 1, pp. 3–11.

p. 204
"Richard Serra. Torqued Ellipse IV.
1998: Moma." *The Museum of Modern
Art*, https://www.moma.org/audio/
playlist/236/3051.

p. 206
Hesson, Robert. "Valerio Olgiati - Frame
Construction." *Northern Architecture*, 7 Jan.
2022, https://www.northernarchitecture.
us/frame-construction/valerio-olgiati.
html.

p. 208
See "In Conversation with Christian Kerez"
within this book.

p. 220
"Institute of Contemporary Art."
DS+R, https://dsrny.com/project/
institute-of-contemporary-
art?index=false§ion=projects.

p. 232
Sveiven, Megan. "Ad Classics: Sendai
Mediatheque / Toyo Ito & Associates."
ArchDaily, 9 Mar. 2011, https://www.
archdaily.com/118627/ad-classics-sendai-
mediatheque-toyo-ito.

p. 234
"Phæno Science Centre." *AKT II*, 2 Sept.
2021, https://www.akt-uk.com/projects/
phaeno-science-centre/.

p. 250
Hertzberger, Herman, and John Kirkpatrick.
*Architecture and Structuralism: The
Ordering of Space*. Nai010 Publishers,
2015.

p. 254
Koolhaas, Rem, et al. *Project Japan:
Metabolism Talks...* Taschen, 2011.

p. 270
Corbo, Stefano. *From Formalism to Weak
Form: The Architecture and Philosophy of
Peter Eisenman*. Routledge, 2020.

IMAGE CREDITS

All photos, and diagrams were produced by PRAUD, unless otherwise noted.

p. 9
Berlin-Tokyo|Tokyo-Berlin, Toyo Ito, Berlin, Germany. 2006, Courtesy of Toyo Ito and Associates

p. 11
Sendai Mediatheque, Toyo Ito, Sendai, Japan. 2001, Courtesy of Toyo Ito and Associates

p. 13
National Taichung Theater, Toyo Ito, Taichung, Taiwan. 2016, Courtesy of Toyo Ito and Associates

p. 23
Google Image Search Engine, 2021

p. 29
"Essai Sur L'architecture", Marc-Antoine Laugier, Paris, France. 1753

p. 31
Le Précis Des Leçons D'architecture Données À L'école Polytechnique, Jean-Nicolas-Louis Durand, Paris, France, 1802

p. 63
Animate Form, Greg Lynn, CCA, Canada. 1997–2001, Courtesy of Greg Lynn

p. 67
Kate Scardifield, SOFT TOPOLOGIES, 2018, (Detail) Adaptable Sculpture in One Variation, Chevron pleated spinnaker cloth, eyelets, powder coated steel, 120 × 148 cm (full extension), Photo: Robin Hearfield

p. 69
White Elephant, Bureau Spectacular, Louisville, USA. 2011

p. 73
Architectural Alphabet, Johann David Steingruber, 1773

p. 75
Von Ledoux Bis Le Corbusier. Ursprung Und Entwicklung Der Autonomen Architektur, Emil Kaufman, Verlag Dr. Rolf Passer, 1933

p. 77
Siteless, François Blanciak, MIT Press. 2008

p. 79
Evolution of City Building under Zoning Law, Hugh Ferris, New York City, USA. 1922

p. 105
Nieuw Stadscentrum Tel Aviv, Bakema van den Broek, Tel Aviv, Israel. 1963, Courtesey of Het Nieuw Einstituut

p. 109
Ad Phoenix/Arizona, Peter Trummer, Berlage Institute, The Netherlands, 2008

p. 266
National Taichung Theater, Toyo Ito, Taichung, Taiwan. 2016, Courtesy of Toyo Ito and Associates

CREDITS

EDITED BY:
Rafael Luna
Dongwoo Yim

ESSAYS BY:
Anthony Vidler
Toyo Ito

INTERVIEWS WITH:
Ben van Berkel
Greg Lynn
Christian Kerez
Toyo Ito

DRAWINGS: (All diagrams by PRAUD unless noted)
Rafael Luna
Dongwoo Yim
ChaerinYu
Hyeonju Lee
Jeongseok Lee
Lorenza Esposito
Kyeongjun Na
Subin Lee
Youmin Kim

INDEX

Note: *Italic* page numbers refer to figures.

Abraham, R. 128
absolute form 116, *117*
adopted form 112, *113*
AD Phoenix/Arizona *125*
Albert, E. 214
Alsop, W. 146, 156, *157*
Ambasz, E. 46
Amore Pacific Headquarters, Seoul, Korea
 102, *103*
Animate Form 70, *71*, *78*, *79*
Aravena, A. *277*
Araya, M. 12, *15*
Architectural Alphabet 88, *89*
Architectural Association (AA), London 45;
 Maison Dom-ino, Venice, Italy 24, 32,
 38–39, *39*, *178*
Architectural Design 52
Architectural Review 49
Architecture Is Everywhere, Chicago,
 USA *279*
Architettura e la città 52
Argan, G. C. 22, 43; "On the Typology
 of Architecture" ("Sul concetto di
 tipologia architecttonica") 24, 52
Arnhem Central Station 67
Atlantis Sentosa Resort 71
Aureli, P. V.: *Possibility of an Absolute
 Architecture, The* 116
avant-garde 168
Aymonino, C. 43, 52

Baird, G.: "'La Dimension Amoureuse'
 in Architecture" 48; "Meaning in
 Architecture" 47, 48
Bakemas, J. 120
Balmond, C. 12, 15
Banham, R. 51
Baroque Architecture 178
Barthes, R. 48
Becher, B.: water towers 40, *41*
Becher, H.: water towers 40, *41*
Behavioral Environmental Design 45
Bentham, J. 53–54
Berkeley Art Museum, California 212
Bettini, S. 52
Bill, M. 44
bio-technical determinism 47
Bjarke Ingels Group 96
Blanciak, F.: "Siteless" 92, *93*
Bobardi, L. 224
body topologies *87*

Bofill, R. 21, 80
Boullée, É-L. 116; Palace of Justice 58–59
Brasilia TV Tower, Brasília, Brazil 222, *223*
Brugge pavilion, Belgium 194, *195*
Burnham Pavilion 68, *69*
Burnham Pavilion, UN Studio, Chicago,
 USA 210, *211*

Cache, B. 70, *72*
Candela, F. 200
Casa da Musica 136
Cathedral of Santa Maria del Fiore 22
CCTV, Beijing, China 154, *155*
Center for Creative Arts 220
Centro de Exposicoes do Centro
 Administrativo da Bahia 186
Chaley, J. 186
Changing Room, The 68
Chicago Cultural Center 278
Chipperfield, D. 103
Chu, K. 73
CIAM see Congrès International
 d'Architecture Moderne (CIAM)
city, as topologies 124–125
City Hall project, Trieste 58
City History Museum, MAS, Neutelings
 Riedijk Architects, Antwerp, Belgium
 260, *261*
City of Culture of Galicia 146
closed context 102–103
Cloud Project *145*
collage city 57
collective form 118–123
College City, Gangnam, Seoul, Korea *113*
Colquhoun, A. 22, 24, 43–52; "Typology
 and Design Methods" 44, 47, 48
column: expression 222, *223*; flat 238,
 239; frame 224, *225*; modular
 slab 240, *241*; object 242, *243*;
 programmable 234, *235*; room 236,
 237; spatial 232, *233*; strapping 226,
 227; table 228, *229*
"Commercialized Residences" 329
compositional form 118, *119*
Congrès International d'Architecture
 Moderne (CIAM) 21
connotation 104–105
containment, topologies of 158, *159*
Contemporary Architecture 21, 25; Google
 vs Modern Architecture 28; quandary
 of 22

contextualization 92–93; legal 94–95; urban 96–97
contextual transformation 98–99
continuous slab 216, 217
core: façade 258, 259; infrastructural 254, 255; metabolic 252, 253; obese 260, 261; siamese 248, 249; skewer 244, 245; stretching 246, 247; structuralist 250, 251; tentacle 256, 257
Costa, L. 222, 223
coursing 276, 277
courtyards 114, 115
Crystal Palace 54
Cullen, G. 42
Culot, L. K. M. 42

Daum Headquarters, Mass Studies, Jeju, Korea 241
Decaspei, G. 206, 207
decon-textual 180, 181
De Coulanges, F. 62
De-Form 80, 81
Delevoy, R. 42
denotation 104–105
Dentsu Headquarters, Tokyo, Japan 226, 227
De Quincy, A.-C. Q. 24, 40, 43, 52; Dictionnaire historique d'architecture 22
Design Models 69
determinalist functionalism 48
Dewitt Chestnut Apartments, Chicago, USA 191
Dieste, E. 200, 201
dis-orientation 84, 85
Doha Metro Network 69
Dom_ino slab 214, 215
donut 76, 77
Dubai Expo Korean Pavilion, Dubai, UAE 289, 291; three-dimensional structural pattern 292–295, 293–295
Duffy, F. 48
Durand, J.-N.-L.: Le Précis des leçons d'Architecture Données à l'École Polytechnique 36, 37

École royale polytechnique 36
Edo Tokyo Museum, Tokyo, Japan 228, 229
"Education of an Architect: A Point of View," Museum of Modern Art, New York 130
Educatorium, Utrecht, The Netherlands 217
Eisenman, P. 46, 72, 73, 142, 146, 180, 268
elements 24–25, 32; programmatic 134, 135; separation of roles by 182, 183
"Embryological House" project 78
emerging grid 16, 17
eternal architecture versus coded professional architecture 61
ETH the Blue House 166

Euclidean geometry 10
Eyebeam Museum of Art and Technology, DS+R, New York, USA 220, 221

Fabbrica Automazione Trasporti e Affini (FATA) 186
façade: core 258, 259; design 176, 177; expression of structure 188, 189; function of 188, 189; interchangeable 178, 179; structural 188, 189
Familistery 54
Farnsworth House 68, 210
FATA see Fabbrica Automazione Trasporti e Affini (FATA)
Feast of Flower, A, Seoul, Korea 231
Ferris, H. 95
figure-ground 140, 141
figure no ground 156, 157
figure over ground 300–303, 301–303
figure-sky 152, 153
Fisac, M. 26
flat column 238, 239
fluid body architectures 12–13
fluid surface 210, 211
fluid walls 212, 213
flying architecture 156
Ford, H. 60
Fordist approach to mass production 20
form 24–25, 32; absolute 116, 117; adopted 112, 113; collective 118–123; compositional 118, 119; found 128, 129; group 122, 123; hybrid 126, 127; megaform 120, 121; over function 130, 131; parts 138, 139; pure 90; as system 136, 137; whole 138, 139
formalism 88
Foucault, M. 53
found form 128, 129
found system 278, 279
Fountain projects 73
four houses 316–319, 316–319
Fourier, C. 54
four walls 206, 207
frame: column 224, 225; tube 190, 191; urban 154, 155
Frampton, K. 46, 50; "Towards a Critical Regionalism: Six Points for an Architecture of Resistance" 21
free-form shells 13
French fries sandwich 304–307, 305–307
Friedman, Y. 50, 144, 145, 156
Fujimoto, S. 279
functional determinism 43
functionalism 45

Gabetti e Isola 142
Geddes, R. 46
Gehry, F. 72, 180
gentrification 56
Glass, P. 68

Godin, J.-B. A. 54
Gombrich, E. 48; *Meditations on a Hobby Horse* 47
Google: Contemporary Architecture vs Modern Architecture 28; image search engine 29
Gothic architecture 22, 28
Grand Pont Suspendu, Fribourg 186
Graves, M. 21, 46
"GRIN" 13
groundfigure 142, 143
grounds 146, 147
groundscape 148, 149
ground stacking 274, 275
group form 122, 123
Guggenheim Museum 204
Gwangju Library 289, 291; structural ground 296–299, 297–299

Habitat 67, Montreal, Canada 262, 263
Hadid, Z. M. 28, 146, 180
Hecker, Z. 265
Hejduk, J. 130
Helsinki Public Library, Helsinki, Finland 288, 290; vertical third space 313–315
Hemeroscopium House, Ensamble Studio, Madrid, Spain 267
Herzog, J. 20, 166
Herzog and De Meuron, 1111 Lincoln Road, Miami, USA 20, 172, 239
Heydar Aliyev Center, Baku 28
Highrise Building, Sparkplug Project 129
Hillside Terrace, Tokyo, Japan 122, 123
Himmelblau, C. 180
Holiday Home 68
holistic ornament 198, 199
Holl, S. 26, 156; Simmons Hall, Cambridge, USA 193; "Y House" 88
Hollein, H. 128, 129
Holy Redeemer Church, Tenerife, Spain 237
horizontal third space 308–311, 309–311
Hotel de Beauvais 140
Hotel Liesma, Jurmala, Latvia 288, 290; figure over ground 301–303
Hunstanton School 50
hybrid form 126, 127
hyperbolic paraboloids 200, 201

I-beam stacking 268, 269
Iglesia Del Cristo Obrero, Atlántida, Uruguay 201
Ikeda, M. 12
industrialization 54
infrastructural core 254, 255
Innovation Center UC, Santiago, Chile 277
Institute of Contemporary Arts, Boston 220
in-tension 186, 187

intent: massing 320–321; topology and 86, 87
interchangeable façades 178, 179
Interlace, The, OMA, Singapore 275
interlocking 272, 273
internet of things 71
Internet of Value 71
Irarrazaval, S.: "2Y House" 88
Isozaki, A.: "City in the Air" 144

Jencks, C.: *Complexity and Contradiction in Architecture* 48; "Glossary of Semiological Terms" 49; "Meaning in Architecture" 47, 48; "Semiology and Architecture" 49
Jenks, C. 166
Jeonghwa, C. 230, 231
Jewish Museum, Berlin 110, 111
Jonas, W. 156

Kahn, F. 190, 198
Kahn, L. 45, 186, 250, 251
Kaku, M. 71
Kaufmann, E.: *Von Ledoux Bis Le Corbusier Ursprung Und Entwicklung Der Autonomen Architektu* 90, 91
Kengo Kuma 20
Kerez, C. 166–174, 209
Kikutake, K. 229
Kitchen Tower XDGA, Anderlecht, Belgium 258, 259
Koetter, F. 140; *Collage City* 112
Kohler, W. 49
Koolhaas, R. 38, 154, 180
Krier, L. 25, 51, 57, 59
Kudo, M.: "Function of the Ornament, The" 30
Kurokawa, K. 254, 255

Laarman, J. 282
Labatut, J. 46
La Pagoda, Madrid, Spain 203
La Pagoda building 26
Laugier, M.-A. 11–12, 65; "Essay on Architecture" ("Essai sur l'Architecture") 34, 35; primitive hut 24, 34–36, 53
lawn third space 162, 163
Le Corbusier 20, 45, 55, 56, 166; Five Points of Architecture 176, 182; Maison Domino 24; *Vers une Architecture* 60–61; Villa la Roche, Paris, France 177; Villa Savoye 22, 146; Ville Radieuse 118, 119
Ledoux, C. N. 90
legal contextualization 94–95
Le Précis des leçons d'Architecture Données à l'École Polytechnique 37

Levi-Strauss, C. 62; *Structural Anthropology* 47–48
Libeskind, D. 110, 111, 180
Lima, J. F. 186
Lissizky, E. 156
lofting 202, 203
Log H, Mount Fuji Architects Studio, Tokyo, Japan 269
London Olympic Dome 72
Los Manantiales 200
Lotus 52
Louisville Children's Museum, Louisville, USA 288, 290, 305–307
Luna, R. 166–174
Luxor Theatre, Rotterdam, The Netherlands 218, 219
Lynn, G. 70–74; *Animate Form* 70, 71, 78, 79; "Embryological House" project 78
Lyon 172

machine architecture 53
Maison Dom-ino, Venice, Italy 24, 32, 38–40, 39, 68–69, 178, 184
Maker Chairs 282, 283
Maki, F. 118, 120, 122, 328, 329; Hillside Terrace, Tokyo, Japan 122, 123
Maldonado, T. 46, 48, 52; *Design, Nature, and Revolution: Toward a Critical Ecology* 44–45; *La Speranza progettuale: Ambiente e società* 44
Market Hall, Rotterdam, The Netherlands 160, 161
Martin, Sir L. 43
MASP, São Paulo, Brazil 225
mass housing 53, 54
massing: intent 320–321; strategy 322–323
material logic 194, 195
Max Reinhardt Haus, Berlin, Germany 153
Maxwell, R. 49
McHale, J. 49
McLuhan, Marshall 72
megaform 120, 121
Menis, F. 237
Mercedes-Benz Museum, Stuttgart 69
Meredith, M. 270
metabolic core 252, 253
Michelangelo 61
Mikimoto Building, Tokyo 198, 199, 330
Millennium Park, Chicago 210
Miller, J. 49, 50
Mirador Housing, Madrid, Spain 114, 115
Möbius House 66, 68
modernism 20, 28, 53, 59, 60, 166, 168, 178, 183, 184, 185, 328–332; postmodernism 20–21, 58, 108, 166, 168, 329
modern system, mutations of 185
modular slab column 240, 241
modular stacking 262, 263

modular system 264, 265
Mondadori, S. 186
Moneo, R. 22; "On Typology" 24, 40
Morphemes 329
Moussavi, F.: "Function of the Ornament, The" 30
mug 76, 77
Munari, B.: Scatola di Architettura 104, 105; *Supplemento al Dizionario Italiano* 106, 107
Muratori, S. 43
Museo Internacional Del Barroco, Toyo Ito, Puebla, Mexico 212, 213
Museum Internacional del Barroco 330
Museum of Image and Sound 220
Music Theatre, Graz 67
MVRDV: Mirador Housing, Madrid, Spain 114, 115

Nakagin Capsule Tower, Tokyo, Japan 255
National Taichung Theater, Toyo Ito, Taichung, Taiwan 14, 26, 285, 285
Neo-Rationalism 44
Neue Nationalgalerie 10, 12
Neumann, A. 26, 264, 265
New Amsterdam Plein and pavilion 68
New Deichman Main Library, Oslo, Norway 272
New York Museum of Modern Art: "Architectural Fantasies" 128
Niemeyer, O. 186
Niemeyer Museum 186
"Nieuwe Zakelijkheid" (New Objectivity or New Pragmatism) 69
Nieuw Stadscentrum Tel Aviv, Tel Aviv, Israel 121
9 SQUARE Exercise 131
Nouvel, J. 198

O-14, RUR 198, 199
obese core 260, 261
object column 242, 243
oblique 150, 151
OCAD 156
Ochoquebradas House 100, 101
Olgiati, V. 256, 257
OMA 20; Dom_ino slab 214, 215; Educatorium, Utrecht, The Netherlands 217; Interlace, The, Singapore 275; Luxor Theatre, Rotterdam, The Netherlands 218, 219; Seattle Central Library, Seattle, USA 134, 135
OMV H2 House 72
one wall 208, 209
open context 100–101
ornament: holistic 198, 199; structural 196, 197
Otto, F. 67

Palace of Justice 58–59
Palacio da Alvorada 186
Palazzo Borghese, Rome, Italy 140, *141*
Palazzo Farnese, Rome, Italy 140
Panopticon 53, *54*
parametricism 21, 28
Parent, C. 150, *151*
Pawley, M.: *Architecture versus Housing* 53
Perm Museum XXI, Perm, Russia 256, *257*
Pevsner, N. 49
Phaeno Science Centre, Wolfsburg,
Germany 235
Phalanstery 54, 60
Physical Environmental Design 45
Pichler, W. 128
PMT Building, Nagoya 328, *329*
postmodernism 20–21, 58, 59, 166, 168, 329
PRAUD 70–74, *171*
prefab stacking 266, *267*
preform stacking 270, *271*
Price Tower, Bartlesville, USA 246, *247*
primitive hut 24, 34–36, 53
productivism 56
programmable column 234, *235*
programmatic element 134, *135*
Project for Forum for Music, Dance and
Visual Culture Centre, Ghent 16
Project for Taichung Metropolitan Opera
House 16
pure form 90

Quaroni, L. 43

ribbon 220, *221*
Richards Medical Research Laboratories,
Philadelphia, USA 250, *251*
Rogers, E. 43
Rogers, R. 328, *329*
room column 236, *237*
Rosenthal Center for Contemporary Art 146
Rossi, A. 24, *25*, 43, 52, 56–59; *Architecture
of the City, The* 62
Rowe, C. 42–43, 60, *61*, 140; *Collage
City* 112
Roy and Diana Vagelos Education
Center 220
Rule of Engagement 166–174
rules of the game 166
RV Prototype 72
Rykwert, J. 43, 52; "Sitting Position – a
Question of Method, The" 48

Safdie, M. 263
Sample, H. 270
SANAA 98, *99*
San Cataldo Cemetery, Modena, Italy 33
Santiago de Compostela 142

Sasaki, M. 12
Scardifield, K. 82, *83*
Scatola di Architettura 104, *105*
SC Johnson Wax Research Tower, Racine,
USA 244, *245*
Seattle Central Library, OMA, Seattle, USA
134, *135*
Seattle Public Library 134
Seifert surface 67
semiotics 108–109
Sendai Mediatheque, Toyo Ito, Sendai,
Japan *13*, 233, 330
SEOUL Edu-Carpet, Seoul, Korea 162, *163*
Serpentine Gallery Pavilion, Toyo Ito,
London, UK 15–17, 186, 283–285, *284*
Serra, R. 204, 205
Sharp Center for Design, Toronto, Canada
156, *157*
Sharp Centre 146
Shizuoka Press and Broadcasting Center,
Tokyo, Japan 252, *253*
siamese core 248, *249*
Sifang Art Museum 156
signified 110–111
signifier 110–111
sign language 106, *107*
Simmons Hall, Cambridge, USA 26, *193*
single surface 218, *219*
skewer core 244, *245*
slab: column, modular 240, *241*; continuous
216, *217*; deformation of 330; Dom_ino
214, *215*
socio-political "advocacy" theories 44
socio-spatial schemata 48
soft topologies 82, *83*
Space Salim, Seoul, Korea 289, *291*;
horizontal third space 309–311
spatial column 232, *233*
stacking: ground 274, *275*; I-beam 268,
269; modular 262, *263*; prefab 266,
267; preform 270, *271*
Steingruber, J. D.: Architectural Alphabet
88, *89*
Stirling, J. 49
Stokes, A. 49
Stranded Sears Tower 73
strapping column 226, *227*
stretching core 246, *247*
strip city 57
structural aesthetics 188, *189*
structural façade 188, *189*
structuralist core 250, *251*
structural ornament 196, *197*
suburbanization 56
Sullivan, L. 128
Summerson, Sir J. 43
Synagogue, Negev Desert, Israel 265

system 24–25, 32, 324–325; form as 136, *137*
system of expression 188, *189*

table column 228, *229*
tables 230, *231*
Taipei Performing Arts Center, OMA, Taipei, Taiwan 126, *127*
"Talponia" 142
Tama Art Library 330
Tange, K. 45, 226, *227*, 253, *255*
Taylor, F.W. 60
Team X 42, 55
tentacle core 256, *257*
Theatre Agora 66, *67*
Theatre de Stoep 66, *67*
third space *159*; horizontal 308–311, *309–311*; lawn 162, *163*; production of *326–327*; tunnel 160, *161*; vertical 312–315, *313–315*
"Third Typology, The" 24–26, 32, 42–62
Tod's Omotesando Building 17, 196, *197*, 330; structural analysis 15
Tokyo Project 226
topology 23; blocks 23; body 87; city as 124–125; of containment 158, *159*; and intent 86, *87*; soft 82, *83*
torqued ellipses 204, *205*
Torre Glories, Barcelona 198, *199*
To/Ty diagram *287*
Towada Art Center 98
townscape 42, 57
Toy Furniture projects 73
Toyo Ito Museum of Architecture, Toyo Ito, Imabari, Japan 272, *273*
Trés grande bibliothéque, OMA, Paris, France 134, *135*
Tschumi, B. 180; *Manhattan Transcripts, The* 132
tube frame 190, *191*
TU Delft Library, Mecanoo, Delft, The Netherlands 142, *143*
tunnel third space 160, *161*
Twins, WOJR, Upstate New York, USA *139*
"2Y House" 88
type-solutions 24
typology 22–25

unanchoring architecture 144, *145*
UN Studio 20, 26
urban contextualization 96–97

urban frame 154, *155*
urbanism 55, 56
urban renewal 56

Van Beek, V. B.: Maison Dom-ino, Venice, Italy 24, 32, 38–40, *39*
Van den Broek, B. *121*
Van der Rohe, M. 10–12, 45, 68, 116
Vanke Center 156
Venice School of Architecture 52
Venturi, R. 328; *Learning from Las Vegas* 108, *109*
Vers une Architecture 60–61
vertical third space 312–315, *313–315*
Vidler, A. 22; "Third Typology, The" 24–26, 32, 42–62
Villa la Roche, Paris, France *177*
Villa NM 66
Villa Savoye 22, 146
Villa Wilbrink 66
Ville Radieuse 118, *119*
Virilio, P. 150
Vitrahaus, Herzog and de Meuron, Weil am Rhein, Germany 271

wall(s): fluid 212, *213*; four 206, *207*; one 208, *209*; spacing 204, *205*
Walled Gardens, Seoul 116, *117*
water towers 40, *41*
West 57 Building 96, *97*
White Elephant, Bureau Spectacular, Louisville, USA *85*
White U 328, *329*
Wimbledon House 328
Wittkower, R. 61
Wright, F. L. 204, 245, 247
WZB, James Stirling, Berlin, Germany 132, *133*

Xenakis, Y. 50

"Y House" 88
Yim, D. 166–174
Yokohama International Passenger Terminal, FOA, Yokohama, Japan 148, *149*
Youturn Pavilion 68

Zaha Hadid Architects 20, *21*
zoning law: evolution of city building under 94, *95*
Zumthor, P. 20